Sources in History
Source-based exercises in British and European history

The Twentieth Century

Malcolm L. Pearce
York Sixth Form College

Bell & Hyman

Published by
BELL & HYMAN LIMITED
Denmark House
37–39 Queen Elizabeth Street
London SE1 2QB

British Library Cataloguing in Publication Data

Pearce, Malcolm L.
 The twentieth century.
 1. Europe—History—20th century—
 Examinations, questions, etc.
 I. Title   II. Series
 907'.6   D424

 ISBN 0-7135-2625-4

Designed by Bob Wright and Alan Hamp
Cover by Colin Lewis

Typeset in Great Britain by MS Filmsetting Ltd, Frome, Somerset

Printed and bound in Great Britain at The Bath Press, Avon.

Contents

Note to teachers

Not many years ago, the work of the historian was about as divorced from history taught in schools as one could get. Perhaps a 'revolution' in teaching methods and approaches is too grandiose a phrase for the initiatives that have brought the common acceptance of skills and source-based history, not only in the classroom but also in the examination room. Certainly the moves that have been made are ones in the right direction. The trepidation of examination boards and teachers, let alone students, in the early days of source-based examination questions has given way to a more refined certainty of the types of questions and sources employed in examinations.

The *Sources in History* series[1] aims to:

● Link the nature of historical theory behind the use of sources with questions based on documentary evidence and the syllabuses taught at 'A' level

● Introduce the tasks of the historian and the challenges he/she[2] faces in completing these tasks

● Examine the nature, scope and demands of evidence itself

● Enable students to assess their understanding of the concepts raised, by providing for activities and self-testing at each stage

● Demand from students the types of skills historians must command in order to tackle the problems they encounter

● Relate skills to central issues, topics and personalities in syllabus material, by means of the main exercise sections

● Present stimulating extract material which provides comment on the issues covered

These books were not designed to be original contributions to the debate concerning the philosophy of history. Of necessity some of the questions central to this debate have been raised, especially in those pages dealing with historians' writings and those dealing with the concept of bias. However, no answers have been sought and the ideas raised have been left very open-ended, deliberately, to allow for those interested to pursue them in class discussion.

In fact, I hope these books, and the exercises they contain, will be used as a stimulus to that most valuable of classroom activities—talk between teachers and students about the fascination of history. Quite simply these books are practical in purpose and their conception lay in the desire to introduce 'A' level students to the processes involved in dealing with historical materials of all types. They aim to develop the skills necessary to handle such sources, and to test these skills in a series of exercises highlighting central issues, while reflecting the different 'A' levels examination boards' source-based questions.

[1] *The Nineteenth Century*   Published September 1986
The Twentieth Century   Published September 1986
The Seventeenth Century   In preparation
The Sixteenth Century   In preparation

[2] For the sake of convenience only, the pronoun 'he' has been used for 'the historian' in the main text.

Acknowledgements

My interest in the teaching of source-based history dates from my time as a research student and tutor at Liverpool University. Since then my interest has grown and been heightened by the development of the skills-based approach to history, the initiatives of the various examination boards, and my experience of teaching history in schools.

My colleagues and predecessors have helped considerably, and special thanks go to the late Douglas Collar and Peter Bamford, my own history masters at Taunton's School, Southampton; Dr. Robert Unwin of the Leeds University Department of Education; Geoffrey Stewart, Head of History at the York Sixth Form College; and, Robert Bland, Head of History at Garforth Comprehensive School, Leeds. Successive generations of pupils and students have also lent their help and support, some unwittingly, not only as recipients but also as active educators in their own right, as any teacher will affirm. Caroline Paines and the editorial staff at Bell & Hyman have been a constant stimulus to work and offered help and advice during the writing of these books. North Yorkshire County Council gave me the opportunity to take a term's leave of absence, and Magdalene College, Cambridge extended its generosity, friendship, and resources in allowing me to make maximum use of that opportunity as Walter Hamilton Schoolmaster Fellow Commoner during the Michaelmas Term in 1984.

Finally, my thanks go to my wife and constant supporter who little imagined that married life would entail not only living with a husband but also a seemingly continual stream of ideas for books, typescripts, manuscripts, and all the paraphernalia of history and its teaching—my greatest thanks and debt as always, is to Diana.

The author and publisher are indebted to the following:

For permission to reproduce text extracts:
George Allen & Unwin for two tables from *The Making of the Second World War* by A. P. Adamthwaite and an extract from *Parliamentary Government* by Harold Laski; The Bodley Head for an extract from *Virgin Soil Upturned* by Mikhail Sholokhov; Jonathan Cape and the Executors of the Bernard Pares Estate for two extracts from *My Russian Memoirs* by Bernard Pares and an extract from *The Russian Revolution* by Marcel Liebman translated by Arnold Pomerans; Frank Cass & Co. for material from *Great Britain and the German Navy* by E. L. Woodward; Cassell Ltd for material from *Amritsar* by Alfred Draper and from *The Second World War* Vol. II by Winston Churchill; Curtis Brown for an extract from *The Suez Affair* by Hugh Thomas; The Hamlyn Publishing Group for an extract from *Hitler: A Study in Tyranny* by Allan Bullock; HMSO Books for material from Hansard; Hutchinson for material from *An Ambassador's Memoirs* by Maurice Paléologue and an extract from *Mein Kampf* by Adolf Hitler; David Higham Associates for an extract from *The Twilight of Imperial Russia* by Richard Charque published by OUP; Macmillan Publishers for material from *Life of Neville Chamberlain* by Keith Feiling and from *King George V* by Kenneth Rose; Oxford University Press for material from *The Struggle for Mastery in Europe 1848–1918* by A. J. P. Taylor and from *Empire to Welfare State: English History*

1906–1976 by T. D. Lloyd as well as from *The Russian Empire* by Hugh Seton-Watson; Secker and Warburg for extracts from *The Rise and Fall of the Third Reich* by William Shiner; The International Institute for Strategic Studies for material and tables; Times Newspapers Ltd for two reports on Guernica; Professor A. Ulum for an extract from his book *Stalin: The Man and his Times*; University of Chicago Press for two extracts from *Russia and its Crisis*, by P. Milyorov, ed. T. Riha; A. P. Watt and the Executors of the Estate of Robert Graves for an extract from *Goodbye to All That*; Weidenfeld Publishers for material from *Russia in Revolution* by L. Kochan.

Every effort has been made to contact copyright-holders, but this has not proved possible in every case. The publishers would be pleased to hear from any copyright-holders not acknowledged.

For permission to reproduce illustrations:
Associated Press, p. 26
BBC Hulton Picture Library, pp. 39, 82
Bildarchiv Preussischer Kulturbesitz, Berlin, p. 12
Bridgeman Art Library and DACS, © 1986, p. 19
The British Library, p. 49
HMSO, pp. 13, 17
Macdonald Publishers, p. 23 and the Imperial War Museum, p. 24 (left)
Oxford University Press and *The Sydney Morning Herald*, p. 58
Punch Publications, pp. 39 (top), 48, 56, 74
The Standard, pp. 66, 78, 83
Thames and Hudson Publishers, p. 18
Ullstein Bilderdienst, Berlin, p. 29
The illustration on p. 24 (right) was supplied by the author.

For permission to reproduce examination questions:
The Associated Examining Board, Joint Matriculation Board, Oxford and Cambridge Schools Examination Board, University of Cambridge Local Examinations Syndicate, University of Oxford Delegation of Local Examinations, University of London Schools Examination Board.

The information given in the section 'Examination advice', pp. 33–36, is the sole responsibility of the author and has not been provided or approved by the examination boards.

Section One

The historian at work

Exercise One tests understanding of the tasks facing the historian.

Evidence

Exercises Two and Three test understanding of the nature of evidence and problems arising from the use of evidence.

Sources

Different types of sources encountered by the historian with examples and some of the questions they raise as to their suitability and usefulness as historical evidence. Followed by Exercise Four to test understanding.

Bias and controversy

Bias and controversy in history both in sources and interpretations. Exercise Five contains two examples of bias from British and European history.

Examination advice

Explanation of the types of questions, major pitfalls, and helpful hints in dealing with documentary source-based questions.

The historian at work

When a historian studies a particular event his task is to **find** and **digest** all the available materials concerning that event; to use his historical skills to **put the event in context**; to **explain why it happened**; **why it took the course that it did**; **what resulted from it**; and finally, to **draw valid conclusions** from its occurrence and results. Underlying all these processes is the existence of basic materials which the historian can use, and generally it is not the lack of material that is the challenge for the historian but the immensity of the materials available. Everything that exists has some historical significance, in that it has a past and can therefore tell us something about itself and the times in which it was created. It may well be a unique source and so vital as the only source of evidence about a period, person, or event. It could well be more humdrum, one of many thousand examples of similar or identical sources. It is still, nevertheless, a historical source. However, not all sources are useful all the time and some are obviously more important than others.

Two more tasks for the historian are to **assign usefulness to sources** and to **elicit information from them**. Without doubt some materials are far more useful than others. A computer adventure game will be a useful social and economic historical source for a study of the late twentieth century but it will not be a useful source for the political historian investigating the way people voted in general elections during the same period. Sources that are consulted by historians studying a particular event can only be used if they are relevant to that event. Even here the historian has a choice to make. When studying election results and voting patterns the historian will find the Returning Officers' records useful because they will give him the number of voters. However, far more revealing would be materials relating to why individuals voted the way that they did. In fact, there is a hierarchy within sources making some more important than others. Similarly, some materials make their worth immediately known while others require some thought and work. A politician's diary will give an easily accessible account of particular events while a collection of government statistics may take some time to collate and interpret before any useful information can be obtained.

However, it would be a poor historian who based his judgements on one source of information alone. In the back of his mind should always lurk the question, 'How far can this material be trusted?' The historian must be confident that the materials he is using are genuine and relate to the events or people he is researching. One way of doing this is to **corroborate information** from one source with that obtained from others. Historians must be wary of sources that they feel only give one side of a particular event. Checking information against other sources, and even the works of other historians, is one way to alleviate these fears. In the last analysis, the choice of materials and the use made of them is the responsibility of the historian and it is his judgement and skill that will determine the success of his study.

Exercise One

1 Using the passage opposite, outline the historian's main tasks when dealing with historical materials.

2 (i) Given two topics of study in the twentieth century, *Food* and *Religion,* which of the following sources would be relevant to each?

   a *New Larousse Gastronomique,* 1977
   b EEC agricultural subsidies
   c French anti-Church legislation in the early years of the twentieth century
   d Minutes of the meetings of the Vatican Council
   e A menu from Maxim's restaurant in Paris
   f Soviet government declarations on the status of functioning churches in the USSR

  (ii) Which of the sources given above would be particularly useful for the study of state interference in food prices and Soviet attitudes to religion?

3 How does the historian go about checking the authenticity of his sources?

Evidence

The historian must try to establish as full a picture as possible of his topic of study and to do this he will have to look at all the available information. Historical information comes in two basic forms: **primary** and **secondary**.

Primary information is anything dating from the moment that an event being studied happened. Such information tends to be in the form of first-hand observation and experience of an event which has been captured in writing, sketching, photography, or memory, although each of these types of sources have their own drawbacks, as we shall see later. Secondary sources are much more like textbooks in that they are collections and re-workings of previously established facts. They can be merely descriptions that have been noted, rehashed, added to, deleted from, and finally passed on in some written, drawn, or verbal form. In fact, secondary information can be very close to the date of an event but that all-important aspect of personal observation and experience is missing. Without doubt, primary information provides the best source to work from but secondary information, despite its second-hand nature, can be useful for the sifting of evidence it provides and also for the ideas it contains. In fact, of course, although a source may be primary it might not be useful for the historian's purposes. As we have seen, in Exercise One, a *Larousse Gastronomique* may be very informative about recipes and culinary techniques but will contain little, if anything, about state intervention in the pricing mechanism of food. However, the level of EEC subsidy for agricultural produce will contain much useful information for the historian involved in this study area. Similarly, details of the meeting of the Vatican Council will reveal much about the policies and ideas of the Catholic Church but will not help in a study of the Soviet Government's attitude to religion. The Russian regulations concerning functioning churches will be a useful source for the historian studying Soviet attitudes to religion. So, historical information provides the basis for the historian's work, which is the recognition, selection and arrangement of evidence from the sources in order to pursue his particular study. No matter whether they are primary or secondary, sources must be useful and relevant to the study being undertaken.

Exercise Two

To test your understanding of the ideas introduced in the section above, divide the following sources for the Cuban Missile Crisis of October 1962 into primary and secondary.

a U2 photographs of the missile bases on Cuba taken in October 1962
b *Washington Post*, October 1962
c *Khrushchev Remembers*, by N. S. Khrushchev, translated and edited by S. Talbot, 1973
d *The Missiles of October: The Story of the Cuban Missile Crisis 1962*, E. Abel, 1966
e *Kennedy's Presidential Press Conferences*, David Halberstam, 1978
f Records of the Special Committee of the National Security Council of the United States, established 14 October 1962
g *A Thousand Days: John F. Kennedy in the White House*, Arthur M. Schlesinger Jnr, 1965
h *The Cuban Missile Crisis 1962*, Malcolm Pearce, 1983

At first sight, the exercise above may appear to be very straightforward. However, some points may have occurred to you while doing this exercise, making it more complicated than it first seemed.

Firstly, Khrushchev memoirs, source **c**, might appear to be primary information—but has translation and editing in 1973 impaired this source's value? Similarly, one could well comment on the time-lapse between the events in 1962 and the appearance in translation of these memoirs. Has this too devalued this source's usefulness as historical information and by implication the validity of any evidence that this source might contain?

Secondly, are all primary sources equally worthwhile or important to the historian? The answer to this question must be 'No'. Given a free choice, the historian will opt for some primary sources in favour of others. For instance, he may give more weight to a first-hand account of actions taken and decisions made, as is contained in source **f**. These records of the deliberations made during the crisis represent direct and pertinent information for the events under study. The *Washington Post*, a well-respected newspaper, will also be useful. However, due to the seriousness of the threat raised by the Cuban missile bases much of the newspaper copy relied on official government information and speculation and hence this source may be of less value. Similarly, the collection of President Kennedy's press conferences may well contain some information of importance. However, the historian needs to bear in mind that this material was edited many years after the dates of the conferences and that a time-consuming sifting process will have to take place before any possible relevant evidence may be apparent. The information available to historians can be 'seeded', with the historian exercising a preference for the most authentic and relevant of the primary sources of material available to him. As we have already discovered, a source must be relevant to a historical study. Peripheral comments may help, but it is often the first-hand thoughts of individuals involved in historical actions that are the most important.

Thirdly, the historian must be concerned about the truthfulness of the sources he is using. He must be certain that they were produced at the time of an event, that they give a truthful account of events, and can be authenticated by other sources if possible. For example, the U2 spyplane photographs that revealed the Cuban bases were rejected by the Russians as fakes in the first instance, but subsequent events suggested that there were missiles and bases on Cuba. Reliability of sources is another key factor in the historian's dealings with source materials. For instance, all but one of the sources listed is English or American and there are no sources giving a Cuban view. Although these sources may be truthful, it is more than possible that a particular side of events of October 1962 is being presented. At the very least, comparable Soviet sources should also be used for such a study. Fully reliable sources including primary and corroborated accounts from dispassionate observers are far preferable to secondary and uncorroborated accounts from biased observers.

Now that these particular problems have been raised, test your appreciation and understanding of the way in which sources can be graded on grounds of usefulness, relevance, and reliability for their potential use as historical evidence.

Exercise Three

1   The sources listed below relate to the life and times of Leon Trotsky, the great Russian revolutionary leader. Assume that you are making a study of Trotsky's opinions about *the course of the Revolution in Russia*. Order the sources given into primary and secondary and then list them in order of usefulness for the study you have to undertake:

    a   Trotsky's private correspondence with his daughter Zina, 1929–40
    b   Isaac Deutscher, *The Prophet Armed: Trotsky 1879–1921*, 1954
    c   Trotsky's household accounts folders in the Trotsky Archive, Harvard University
    d   Leon Trotsky, *Diary in Exile*, 1958
    e   Isaac Deutscher, *The Prophet Outcast: Trotsky 1929–1940*, 1963
    f   Leon Trotsky, *The Revolution Betrayed*, 1937

2   The sources listed below refer to the era of the first of the Dreadnought class of ships, *HMS Dreadnought*, which was built in 1906 in Britain. Your task is to order the sources, in exactly the same way as above, firstly on the basis of whether they are primary or secondary, and then by usefulness, but this time for a study of *the technical assessment of the Dreadnought*.

    a   A portfolio of photographs of British shipyards for the year 1906
    b   *The Times*, 1906–07, accounts of *HMS Dreadnought's* trials
    c   R. Hough's biography of John Fisher, *First Sea Lord, (1904–1910 and 1914–1918)*, 1969
    d   Construction plans and drawings for *HMS Dreadnought*, 1905
    e   Parliamentary debates on the strategic importance of Dreadnought class vessels, 1908–09
    f   Admiralty papers, 1906–07

Sources

By now you may appreciate the enormous variety of historical material available for study: government reports, Acts of Parliament, written extracts for private and public consumption, speeches, tables, graphs, maps, prints, paintings, illustrations, cartoons, and artefacts. All of these are examples of the types of historical information encountered by the historian, but although they all serve the same function the historian cannot treat them all in the same way. With some he has to be particularly careful because they have their own idiosyncracies when the historian tries to analyse and use them.

Written and printed sources

The most common of all historical sources are written sources but in this simple category the tasks facing the historian are great. We have already seen how historians might value some sources more highly than others but although a manuscript, or handwritten, source is most sought after there are still other considerations, such as:

Legibility   Simply, is the source readable?

Authenticity   Is the source an original, a copy, or a printed transcription open to editing?

Usefulness   Is the source merely a household note, a personal letter, or an authoritative statement concerning a major event or personality?

Printed sources such as **government papers** also have their difficulties—is all the information being made available in the source; has the typescript been edited for lack of space, security reasons, or policy motives; and is the source giving merely one point of view? The same questions can be raised when dealing with **newspapers** because they too suffer from the lack of quality of the reporting, editorial decisions, and the integrity and reliability of the reporter, his sources of information, and sometimes censorship. Much the same can be said of other printed sources such as **biographies** and **books** in general, each will reflect its author's interpretations of evidence and events and the historian must be very careful in using such sources to always have in his mind the question, 'how far is this document reliable as an historical source?' Finally, **posters** and **handbills** bring the greatest problem of using written sources to the fore because they are invariably trying to persuade, give one point of view, or are merely addressing the already committed. The example below has all the elements of the propagandist's art. It is a Nazi poster with a simple but forceful message: 'Marxism dies in Order that (National) Socialism can live'. The

From: Bildarchiv Preussischer Kulturbesitz

obvious appeal to the German worker is there but so is the implication that Marxism is Jewish with the Star of David inserted in the centre of the Red Star of Bolshevism. Although this is a difficult source to assess, it is nevertheless an important one, especially from the point of view of attitudes and the Nazi Party propaganda machine.

Maps

Maps are less frequently used as historical sources but in fact are most valuable, and contain a large variety of information on a number of historical subjects. The example given below locates the levels of infant mortality in the county boroughs of England and Wales for 1931. The symbols relate to the extent of the problem of infant mortality in these administrative units. The clustering of the worse levels of infant mortality in the North-east and the counties of Lancashire and Yorkshire would suggest that the living conditions leading to infant mortality, as well as dietary considerations and wage levels, were not sufficiently high in these areas to

Infant mortality (q_0 parts per thousand) for the county boroughs of England and Wales, 1931

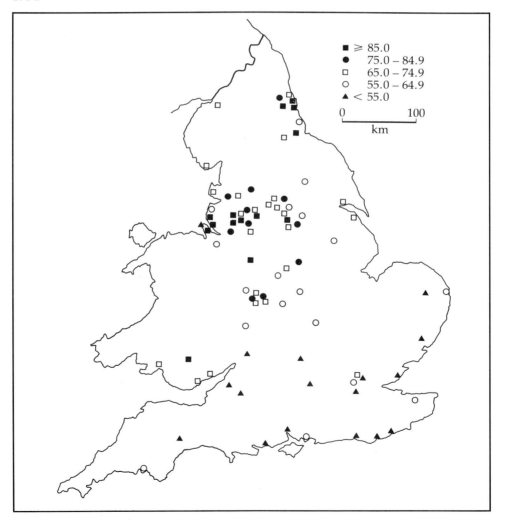

From: Registrar General's *Annual Statistical Review for England and Wales*, 1930, 1931 and 1932; *Population Census of England and Wales*, 1931

overcome the problems leading to early death amongst the young. On the other hand, those county boroughs away from the industrial areas appeared to be able to cope with problems attendant in the early years of life and so their levels of infant mortality were considerably lower than those of the industrial north. Of course, at the moment all these suppositions are open to criticism and will remain so until corroborative evidence has been located.

Statistical material

The extent and variety of statistical material available to the historian makes it an important source of historical information but one that appears in a variety of forms: **tables**, **graphs**, and more recently **computer print-out**. These types of sources are approached in exactly the same way as written sources, that is, with care and a questioning mind. In the same way that written sources have to be checked, authenticated, analysed, and used, so do statistical sources.

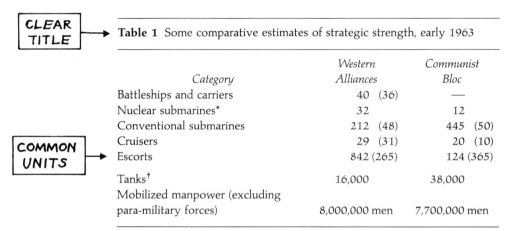

CLEAR TITLE →

Table 1 Some comparative estimates of strategic strength, early 1963

Category	Western Alliances	Communist Bloc
Battleships and carriers	40 (36)	—
Nuclear submarines*	32	12
Conventional submarines	212 (48)	445 (50)
Cruisers	29 (31)	20 (10)
Escorts	842 (265)	124 (365)
Tanks†	16,000	38,000
Mobilized manpower (excluding para-military forces)	8,000,000 men	7,700,000 men

COMMON UNITS →

Ships in reserve are shown in brackets. *Includes both missiles and hunter submarines. †Includes many obsolescent types.

From: Military Balance 1962–63, International Institute for Strategic Studies

The table as presented raises a number of points:

● Is the title clear enough?

● Are the units used in the table common to all parts of the table?

● If yearly intervals have been chosen are the periods to a selected standard?

● Are there any apparent reasons for choosing the years in question?

So far our table looks fairly competent but it is as well to check these in all tables to make sure that everything is in order. However, if we begin to question the information then we see that a picture of only conventional weapons is revealed. Although nuclear submarines are mentioned, all other types of strategic nuclear weapons have been omitted but we need to know these levels of armament before we can make a reasonable assessment of the relative positions of Western Alliance and Communist Bloc countries in 1963.

Table 2 Some comparative estimates of strategic strength, early 1963

Category	Western Alliances	Communist Bloc
ICBMs (over 2,000 miles range)	450–500	75 +
MRBMs (700–2,000 mile range)	250	700
Long-range bombers (over 5,000 mile range)	630	200
Medium-range bombers (over 2,000 mile range, including major carrier-based aircraft)	1,630	1,400

From: ibid.

This second table, the information of which could have been included in the first table, gives us a fuller picture of the relative strengths of the Western Alliances and Communist Bloc countries' military standing in all types of weapons in the early part of 1963. Both conventional and nuclear weapon levels have been included and the historian can make a more valid and hopefully useful evaluation of relative strengths.

If the information presented in Table 1 was the only information used, a distorted view would be given of the Western Alliances and Communist Bloc countries' relative strengths and potential fighting levels in the event of a conflict. Working solely on the information in Table 1, it seems as if the two sides are fairly evenly matched, with the Western Alliance having an advantage at sea outweighed by the Communist Bloc superiority in tanks. However, using all the information available in *both* tables then a different picture emerges, showing the Western Alliances enjoying a considerable superiority in the delivery of nuclear warheads from long range both by missile and airplane. Although the Communist Bloc has some numerical advantage in medium range missiles this does not off-set the Western Alliances' advantages. The advantages enjoyed would appear even more obvious if a historian glanced at a map and looked at the relative distances between the main combatants in the event of a struggle—the USA and the USSR. Obviously, further research would be needed to verify the conclusions reached on the basis of these tables alone.

Graphs are another familiar way of presenting historical material. Information can be conveyed in an easily appreciated visual manner, but just as with tables, and other statistical materials and sources, graphs must be treated with care. Similar questions to those we raised about tables are relevant to graphs: titles must be clear; the intervals used on each axis of the graph should be uniform; and the historian must always be questioning why this particular spread of information has been chosen for graphic display. Other points are important, for example the historian should be aware that the dramatic effect of a graph can be altered merely by changing the scale of the graph. Look at the two examples given below. Both display exactly the same information but, because the scales for each graph are different, one gives a far more vivid representation of the information than does the other. Consequently, it is useful to look at the scales chosen for graphs merely to check that the information is being displayed in a reasonable fashion rather than for dramatic effect.

Graph 1 Population of England and Wales (in millions to nearest 100,000), 1901–81 (1941 omitted)

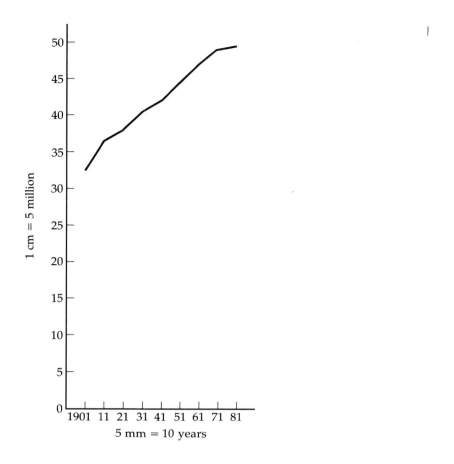

Graph 2 Population of England and Wales (in millions to nearest 100,000), 1901–81 (1941 omitted)

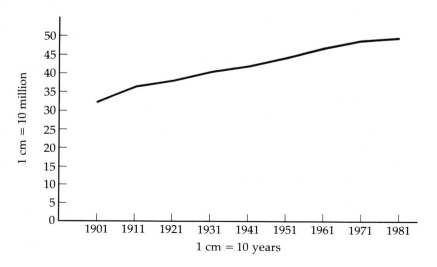

Graph 3 Mean age at first marriage, 1900–74, England and Wales

From: Population Trends 5, Autumn 1976

As with any historical sources, graphs need to be questioned and used. The example above is a graphical display of the mean age of men and women at first marriage between 1900 and 1974. These figures are important because they give an insight into the population growth—because younger mothers have the potential to have more children—and they are also an interesting guide to attitudes to marriage. The graph is particularly intriguing because it shows a complete reversal in attitudes between 1914 and 1939. The onset of war in 1914 persuaded people to delay their marriages, believing the conflict to be a limited one of short duration. This belief was totally shattered when the carnage of the war years took its toll. Hence, the mean age of marriage in 1914 rose sharply because people believed that postponements would be the best temporary solution. However, by 1939, peoples' ideas of war had changed considerably and the terrible losses of 1914–18 were well remembered. People rushed to get married, especially the young, and so the mean age of first marriage for both men and women fell sharply.

Of course, as always, any suppositions made on the basis of this evidence would have to be checked and corroborated.

Cartoons

Cartoons present the historian with some of the most lively of his sources but although they can be full of contemporary comment on historical events they have to be treated very carefully. Cartoons need close study, paying particular attention to captions, the way each character is portrayed, any symbolism that the cartoonist may use—a particular style of dress for instance, an object that a character is carrying, or a particular action that a character is performing.

Look at the cartoon from a French magazine at the turn of the century. The figure of 'William, the little glutton' is that of Kaiser Wilhelm II of Germany. It is interesting that he is shown in military uniform, for although William was a great lover of such costumes, this is also an obvious reference to Germany's military strength and heritage which William did nothing to discourage. He is greedily biting into the globe which is portrayed as an enormous pudding obviously too large for William but he seems intent on taking as big a chunk of the pudding as possible, if not the whole thing. Obviously, this cartoon represents one viewpoint of Germany's actions at this time and the fact that it is French demands that it be treated with caution. However, despite its symbolism and prejudices this cartoon can be as useful an historical source as any other. The historian must just be a little more careful in interpreting and using the information that it contains.

From: *L'Assiette au Beurre*, Paris, 1900

Cartoons as sources tell us a great deal about graphic art, production techniques, drawing styles, and artistic trends in general; they may even provide further information on dress, use of language, interior decoration, and many other facets of social life. However, political cartoons like the example given do not often directly help the historian even though they are primary sources. This is because the cartoon and the message that it carries may well be the view of the cartoonist alone and not necessarily that of the majority of people. This last point also applies to other useful sources of material for the historian, for example illustrations and fictional material.

Illustrations

The historian has to be very careful when using illustrations as a source. Is the image shown a true reflection of events? Was the artist present or was the drawing done from a later description or even his own quick sketches? Was the drawing commissioned and if so, by whom, and why was it commissioned? Already a number of very important questions have been raised as to the validity and usefulness of illustrations and it is the historian's task to distinguish between the true, false, and the biased. Below we have a perfect example, with Pablo Picasso's massive canvas entitled 'Guernica'. The painting symbolises Picasso's feelings and portrays the events of the bombing of Guernica in 1937. However, Picasso was working from reports as he was in Paris at the time of the bombing. Although a modern masterpiece of art and an intense statement of national feeling and grief this particular illustration is of little help if we wished to use it as a source to authenticate other types of materials reporting on the events in Guernica in 1937.

From: The Bridgeman
Art Library. Original
in the Museum of
Modern Art,
New York

Fictional sources

Fictional sources are another rich area of material that the historian can use but when he does he faces major pitfalls. There is even greater need to be careful in the use of fictional sources than there is in the use of illustrations, for they contain not only the seeds of the writer's imagination but all the intricacies of plot imagined by the author for the characters he has created. Fictional sources may contain great insight into a period of history but they can only be thought of as primary sources if they are used to reveal information about the time in which they were written as opposed to the time in which they are set. Moreover, authors, especially those writing about their contemporary world, can reveal all sorts of insights into the society in which they live, and can be some of the most potent sources for giving a 'feeling' for an age. However, equally obviously, they too require a great deal of authentication and testing for reliability—even fictional sources based on real events have to be treated with the greatest caution.

In the extract below, Sholokhov gives an interesting description of the Collectivisation programme's problems in Russia after the Revolution. He outlines the peasants' antipathy for Collectivisation and the ways by which they tried to avoid the process itself sometimes by simply hiding from the bureaucrats whose job it was to implement Collectivisation. However, before one could think of using this as a source it would be necessary to check and verify it with other sources of the period describing and explaining the same events.

> From the beginning of their activities it was obvious that it was going to be very difficult to get the grain fund collected in the period fixed. All the measures undertaken by the brigade and the local nucleus for the purpose of accelerating its collection met with tremendous opposition from the majority of the collective farm members and the individual farmers. Rumours spread through the village that the grain was being collected to send abroad, there would not be any sowing done that year, and war was expected hourly. Nagulnov called daily meetings, and with the help of the brigade explained the situation, refuted the absurd rumours, threatened with the harshest punishment those caught in 'anti-Soviet propaganda'. But the grain continued to come in extremely slowly. The Cossacks found excuses for going off somewhere away from home early in the morning. They went to the forest for wood, or gathered brushwood. Or they went off with their neighbours to spend the anxious day in some secluded spot, in order to avoid having to answer a summons to the village Soviet or the brigade staff....

Mikhail Sholokhov, *Virgin Soil Upturned*, 1935

Work of other historians

Finally, one of the most intriguing aspects of history is that the historian often finds himself studying and evaluating the work of other historians. Work produced by historians can be sources themselves. This type of source can corroborate suspicions by presenting evidence discovered in a historian's own researches and they can be useful guides to new sources of primary and secondary materials. Most important of all, such writings contain other historians' selections of materials, presentations of their evaluations of these materials, and the final explanations by them of the historical problem with which they are concerned. However, as with all types of sources, those arising out of other historians' works must be treated with caution if not suspicion.

Take, for example, the writings of historians on the causes of the First World War. In 1961 Fritz Fischer put forward a forceful argument to the effect that Germany actively promoted herself as a world power and pursued world interests to such an extent that war, preferably localised, was an acceptable risk. Fischer expanded and extended his ideas to put forward a basic belief in Germany's complete responsibility for ensuring that the events of 1914 resulted in international conflict.

> The Kaiser, the Military leaders, and the Foreign Office insisted in the July crisis that Austria should immediately begin hostilities against Serbia. They agreed with Austria's ultimatum to Serbia which was so sharp that there was the greatest probability that it had to lead to war between the two countries. In this way they consciously risked a continental war of Austria-Hungary and Germany against Russia and France. ... When the Kaiser threatened to show weakness ... Bethmann-Hollweg disregarded him. ... Similarly, the Chancellor rejected or delayed all English attempts at moderation. ... There can be no talk that Bethmann-Hollweg's actions at the beginning and at the height of the crisis were not ruled by destiny or a fateful tragedy but were conscious political decisions....
>
> Fritz Fischer, 'World Policy, World Power, and German War Aims', in H. W. Koch (ed.), *The Origins of the First World War*, 1984

As Fischer sees it, the world was set for international conflict as a result of German preparedness to risk all, including war, to obtain her ends, and Bethmann-Hollweg carries the main responsibility for promoting Germany's aims and guiding her onto the path of war. Fischer believes that the German Chancellor had aims for Germany that could be achieved by war if necessary. However, these pronouncements invited immediate comment from many historians, and most notably from German historians. One, Wolfgang Mommsen, rejected Fischer's arguments:

> ... the government of Bethmann-Hollweg did not at any time until May/June 1914 contemplate the idea of attaining any of its objectives by war ... [Bethmann-Hollweg] stuck to a peaceful policy....
>
> Quoted in, Karl Dietrich Erdmann, 'War Guild Reconsidered: A Balance of New Research', in H. W. Koch (ed.), ibid.

Fischer's critics tend to adopt a completely different view of Germany's war aims and the role of leading politicians in promoting these consistently both before and during the war. In part these differences of opinion can be explained by the work undertaken by each of the historians, the sources available to them, and most importantly their own interpretations of the materials. Much of the controversy in this particular example turns on the interpretations given to Bethmann-Hollweg's so-called 'War Aims Programme' of 9 September 1914. Fischer, who uncovered this particular piece of evidence, uses it as a foundation for his interpretation of events, reading into it a conviction that Germany was pursuing a consistent policy dictated by totally unrealistic and grotesquely megalomaniacal demands and aims. On the other hand, Fischer's critics have commented on his use of material and suggested that this declaration of aims was relevant to the time it was written and is not proof of a consistent German war policy either before 1914 or from 1914 to 1918.

Clearly, how a historian uses his sources and views the events of the past can have a considerable effect on the work he produces and the explanations he gives for historical problems. Who is writing, and what research they have undertaken, can be as important as what is written. After all, historians are as open to the weaknesses of human frailty as any other group of people! The content of some historians' writing can be governed by their views of the historical process. Most believe that historical events have causes and that these causes could be linked in some way. Historical events could be represented by means of a plant's root system with each strand feeding into the society of the day and linking one part of the roots to another and the main plant itself. The plant needs its roots to survive and the roots rely on nutrients from the soil as well as processes taking place in the leaves. In the same way the events of an historical period have causes and these in turn help to create other causes and events.

Some historians would take this process even further and claim that not only are events linked but that they are bound to happen. If a historian does imply this then he is being **deterministic**. This means he believes that the actions of people and the events in history are determined by the society in which they live and occur. These historians believe that there are social forces, about which the individual can do nothing, that dictate the actions and events during the lifespan of each historical period. For example, Marxist historians would tend to view the historical process in this way—it is the economic forces in society and the tensions they cause that will determine what happens in history. Such beliefs could well be represented by a straight line, giving no opportunity for events to take any course of action other than the one which happens.

Other writers have rejected the idea of a pre-ordained sequence of events especially as it appears to leave no room for the role of the individual, the so-called great men and women of the past who influenced events in a fundamental way. They would argue that the 'Napoleons', the 'Elizabeth Is', and the 'Hitlers', influenced the times in which they lived and directed historical events, if only for a short time. These historians have sometimes likened history to the parallel lines of a railway track, or the banks of a river, and by doing so have given their ideas on history a little more flexibility. If one sees history rather like a stream, then there is plenty of scope for movement between the banks, for the flow of the stream to grow stronger and weaker at different times, for the big and small fish to cause disturbances and create big and small ripples on the surface. And, of course, ideas on history and the historical process do not end with just these few. Some thinkers have likened history to a circle, even a helix, where the same problems confront mankind but in different times and different forms. Finally, more recently, some historians have rejected any attempts to find a pattern in past events, or to explain history by reference to one set of ideas, and some have asserted that historical events tend to be the result of a more flexible interaction of unrelated causes as well as the accidental which cannot be predicted.

Not only is it the way historians view their subject that influences what each will write but also factors such as national pride, economic need, social and political pressure, and even government direction. All these have to be considered when the works of other historians are used and, of course, one must be aware that exactly the same pressures and prejudices may eventually show themselves in your own writing.

Having raised some of the numerous problems presented by the variety of historical sources it would be best to confront some of these problems and the exercise below is designed to do just that.

Exercise Four

Study the following sources carefully, paying particular attention to any indications you can find of the date, subject, reliability, and potential usefulness of each source. Then attempt the following exercises:

a   Make a list of possible topics that these sources could be used for by a historian.

b   Order the sources chronologically.

c   Divide the sources up into primary and secondary, bearing in mind that we will be using them to make a detailed study of conditions for soldiers in the First World War.

d   Re-order the sources, rating them on their usefulness for giving the historian information about government control of information relating to conditions at the Front. Why should there be differences between this list and the one compiled for **c** above?

e   Why might the government wish to suppress information about Front Line activities—use evidence from the sources provided for your answer.

f   What evidence is there in the sources of not only suppression of information but also falsification of the conditions endured by soldiers at the Front?

EXTRACT A   Personal account by Pte Dick Wills, 8th K.O.Y.L.I., 1918

... then we de-train, must be getting nearer the front if its within walking distance, we march late into the night until we arrive at some small village, again we are expected, more grub, sleep in a barn full of straw, it rains through the night and the barn roof. We spend a couple of days here getting used to the atmosphere which has changed in
5   some subtle way, we see shells in the mud by the road side, in the ditches, in the fields, from little whiz bangs to big nasty 9.2s. Empty shell cases like huge rifle cartridges, wicker cases like wine bottle covers that the larger type of shell lives in till wanted, clips of cartridges both German and British, till we begin to think we must be getting nearer to the front.
   [Next six lines crossed out by the censor]
10   We relieve a battalion in the front line, their faces tell us what to expect, we don't have long to wait. ... We are not in long before we are ordered out, and as we go we see many who have been less fortunate than ourselves at shell dodging, the post corporal is dead with a piece of shrapnel through the back of his skull, we shed a tear for him, a nice chap, a few yards further on our company officer with a chunk of shell in his belly,
15   we have to step in his life's blood to pass, a sargent is sat on the trench floor, with the officer's head in his lap and holding his hand, he screams curses and then cries for his mother...
   [Next two lines crossed out by the censor]
   and so the grim tale goes on....

From: Private papers, Pte Dick Wills

EXTRACT B   Robert Graves, *Goodbye to All That*, 1929

Executions were frequent in France. I had my first direct experience of official lying when I arrived at Le Havre in May 1915, and read the back-files of army orders at the rest camp. They contained something like twenty reports of men shot for cowardice or desertion; yet a few days later the responsible minister in the House of Commons,
5   answering a question from a pacifist, denied that sentence of death for a military offence had been carried out in France on any member of His Majesty's Forces....

EXTRACT C   *The Huddersfield Daily Examiner*, 1 November 1934. Article on reminiscences of Passchendale, 1917

I doubt whether a man without rifle or equipment could have moved more than a mile in twenty-four hours; the usual system was to put down a duckboard walk along it, and put down another, and if a man slipped off his duckboard he was done for unless someone pulled him out immediately. There was one place where a caterpillar tractor,
5   built for such conditions, slipped off the corduroy road, and it took only four days to disappear in the bog. At another place I remember having an argument as to whether there had been a canal or dry land there before the bombardment began.

EXTRACT D   Personal account by Pte Dick Wills, ibid.

... I prepare myself a funk hole for the night. We are being steadily shelled but not heavily, and I get myself a nice little nest, scooped out and crawl in to see how it fits, when a shell falls close and shakes the top down and half buries me, I scramble out and start again, the scooped out earth forms a barrier for shrapnel should a shell fall in the
5   road. I am not on sentry so settle down to sleep, but am rudely awakened by pouring rain, and find myself lying in a pool of water, soaked through and through and frozen stiff, and of course, no possible chance of getting dry, damn and blast the bloody war ...

From: ibid.

EXTRACT E   German postcard, First World War

From: A. Horne, *Death of a Generation*, Macdonald, 1970

EXTRACT F British poster, First World War

From: The Imperial War Museum

EXTRACT G French postcard, First World War

From: Original in author's possession

Bias and controversy

The last section raised the idea of **bias**. Bias is at one and the same time the joy and bane of the historian. It is the thing that makes the subject ever fresh, opens events to differing interpretation, and presents the historian with some of his greatest challenges. It can also create misunderstandings, difficulties and problems. If he is using sources the historian must detect any bias in them, and if he is writing history the historian must try to avoid bias in his own work. Bias is a slanted view of a personality or event that tends to give one side of the story to the exclusion of others, either intentionally or unintentionally.

As we saw in the last section, bias can apply to all types of historical sources simply because each individual has their own conscious and subconscious prejudices.

Bias may arise from a particular social or political standpoint, from an inability to obtain or appreciate all the available evidence, from a religious belief, and because sometimes being unbiased will result in the loss of money, the loss of a job, or even the loss of one's freedom. In fact, the list is endless. So an appreciation of bias and the way in which it affects the historian's tasks is essential.

Bias can also arise from simple prejudice. Take this view of the Russian revolutionary personality, Leon Trotsky, penned by another famous Russian leader Stalin:

> It is said that Trotsky with his campaign for unity has brought a new current into the affairs of the liquidators. But it is not true. Regardless of all his 'heroic' efforts and terrible 'threats', he has proved himself to be a common noisy champion with faked muscles. . . .
>
> Stalin, in a letter to *Social Democrat*, 12 January 1913

Trotsky, a leading figure in the revolutionary movement and a famous Russian spending much of his time abroad in exile, is being openly criticized by Stalin for his attacks on the Bolsheviks' Fighting Squads with whom Stalin was involved. The attacks continued but it is interesting to note Stalin's attitude to Trotsky on the first anniversary of the Russian Revolution when Trotsky was at the peak of his career and Stalin was, at best, a rising star.

> All practical work in connection with the organisation of the uprising was done under the immediate direction of Comrade Trotsky, the President of the Petersburg Soviet. It can be stated with certainty that the party is indebted primarily and principally to Comrade Trotsky for the going over of the garrison to the Soviet and the efficient manner in which the work of the Military Revolutionary Committee was organised.
>
> Stalin in *Pravda*, October 1918

Issac Deutscher, Stalin's biographer, points out that this message of thanks and congratulations still manages to belittle Trotsky's role in the Revolution by hinting that Trotsky was merely good at carrying out Lenin's ideas. As Deutscher indicated when he claimed that Stalin, '. . . could hurt his rival only with a thorn concealed in a bouquet', (Issac Deutscher, *Stalin*, p. 211), the future dictator of Russia was still too small a fish to criticize Trotsky openly. What Stalin felt able to write about Trotsky was determined by his own position in the revolutionary hierarchy in 1918, and the extract above makes it plain that he was not yet certain of his own position and power to criticize. Not that all the criticism was from one direction. As Stalin hinted in the first extract, he had already been taken to task by Trotsky, at least indirectly. Perhaps the final words should be those of Lenin who knew both men:

> . . . Comrade Stalin has acquired immense power in his hands and I am not certain he will always know how to use this power with sufficient caution. On the other hand Comrade Trotsky . . . is distinguished by his remarkable abilities. Personally, he is no doubt, the most able person in the present Central Committee but he also has excessive self-confidence and is overly attracted by the purely administrative aspect of affairs . . . .
>
> Lenin's 'Testament', 24 December 1922

With such volatile and complex personalities and with so much at stake it is hardly surprising that the historian would come across such prejudiced reports, and this merely serves to show the necessity of obtaining as full a picture as possible of the events and personalities being studied.

The illustration below demonstrates this very point. And, just as portions of illustrations, photographs, and cartoons can be interpreted in different ways, so can portions of written sources. Be aware of the fact that what an artist or writer, and for that matter a historian, chooses to 'show' his readers may not be the complete picture concerning a person or event. The first portion of the illustration below appears to show the Italian dictator, Mussolini, acknowledging the adulation of the crowds. However, the second portion shows him, in fact, walking by military personnel, and there is a clue that all is not as it seems because the armband of the soldier on the right carries the swastika emblem. The full details of that event are only revealed in the third, and complete photograph, where Adolf Hitler is seen marching side by side, but somewhat distant from, Mussolini, who like Hitler is acknowledging the Nazi salute of the parade.

1   2   3   *From:* Associated Press

Each portion of the illustration tells its own story, and has its own relevance, but individually they do not give an approximation to the 'truth' until all is revealed. This is also true of written extracts, and the one that follows gives another example of the need to have as complete a source of evidence as is possible.

Editing quotations, using punctuation to give briefer versions of the essence of a written source, is a favourite historical practice, but it is one that needs to be treated with care because what is left out is often as important as what is included. By careful selection of pieces of information a false or biased impression can be given. In the following example we have the British Prime Minister, Neville Chamberlain, trying to placate Adolf Hitler in 1938, after Hitler had sent him a letter on 27 September concerning Czechoslovakia and Germany's demands on this territory.

Neville Chamberlain to Adolf Hitler, 28 September 1938:

1. After reading your letter I feel certain that you can get all ... of France and Italy, if you desire ....
2. ... I am ready to come to Berlin myself at once to discuss arrangements ... with representatives of France and Italy, if you desire. I feel convinced we can reach agreement in ... a few days ....
3. After reading your letter, I feel certain that you can get all essentials without war,

and without delay. I am ready to come to Berlin myself at once to discuss arrangements for transfer with you and representatives of the Czech Government, together with representatives of France and Italy, if you desire. I feel convinced we can reach agreement in a week. I cannot believe that you will take responsibility for starting a world war which may end civilization for the sake of a few days' delay in settling this long-standing problem.

Full text quoted in William L. Shirer, *The Rise and Fall of the Third Reich*, 1971

As you can see, selecting a portion of an historical source is very dangerous. It must be done with care, maintaining as far as possible a neutral position but not excluding relevant information. Historians have an obligation to avoid all possible misinterpretations. However, with the best will in the world, a historian could well give a particular slant to such an edited paragraph and might, unintentionally, omit valuable information. A case in point comes in version two of the paragraph when 'in a week' has been omitted but the misleading 'a few days' has been left in. Even worse than this is the complete misinterpretation of version one which has Chamberlain agreeing to Hitler's taking possession of France and Italy! This is totally wrong and, of course, as we learn from the final version, Hitler was concentrating on Czechoslovakia at this time.

With all sources, care is the important word. However, as well as being careful, the historian must also make certain that the sources he uses give as full a picture as possible of the studies he undertakes.

This section on bias brings us full circle because bias is a result of the historical process itself. Historical information in all its forms exists to be used, questioned, and analysed by historians. Historians are the ones who 'pick over the bones' of past ages. They select the evidence that matters, arrange it, interpret it, and finally they make their thoughts known. At each of these stages bias can occur.

All of the following can lead to bias:

● The initial choice of the subject or personality to be studied

● The pieces of evidence selected

● The use of each portion of evidence

● The individual historian's own opinions and prejudices

So far, we have looked at all these facets of the historian's world by concentrating on the nature of evidence and the difficulties that exist in dealing with such evidence. As a final exercise to draw all these points together, there follow two separate examples of famous controversial events in twentieth century history. Each example contains a number of sources relating to the particular events and personalities. Some are primary and some secondary but all give part of the story surrounding each event. The questions that precede each parcel of sources are designed to help you assess the evidence presented, make your own judgements, and use these to evaluate assessments made of the events by other historians. You will find bias in these sources but identifying it and coping with it is the great challenge of history.

Exercise Five

1   Below are a number of sources relating to the pre-revolutionary period in Russia and particularly the personal relationships of the Tsar, Tsaritsa, and Gregory Rasputin. Controversy surrounds the question of the ineffectiveness of the Tsar,

particularly from 1915 onwards when he took personal command of the war leaving the court and day-to-day politics to others, and the respective roles of his wife and her adviser, Rasputin. Decisions concerning politics, appointments, and eventually the war administration itself were left to the Empress, and her advisers. There is some uncertainty as to how much influence was exercised by Rasputin and exactly how his influence worked on the Tsar, as opposed to the Tsaritsa who appears to have been very reliant upon her adviser.

Questions

a Study Extracts A, B, C and D.

  (i) What evidence can you find to support the view that Rasputin enjoyed a powerful influence in Russian politics at this time?

  (ii) How does Extract D suggest that Rasputin's influence might grow in the future?

b Study the cartoon, E, and Extracts F, G, and H.
  What evidence is there in the written extracts to suggest that the impression given in the cartoon, of Rasputin's direct control of the Tsar, is misleading?

c Using Extracts I and J, explain Rasputin's hold over the Empress. How might this influence exercised by Rasputin have appeared more total than it actually was?

EXTRACT A Maurice Paléologue, *An Ambassador's Memoirs*, Vol. II, entry for Sunday 29 August 1915

For the first time Rasputin has been attacked by the press. Hitherto the censorship and the police had protected him against newspaper criticism. It is the *Boursse Gazette* which has opened the campaign.

EXTRACT B Bernard Pares, *My Russian Memoirs*, 1931

In the rear, the political situation was getting more and more critical. The summoning of the Duma had been postponed and postponed; the aged Premier, Goremykin, was afraid to meet it and as one now knows it was for this reason, and by the wish of the Empress, that he was displaced (February 1916). It was she who chose his successor
5 directly on the recommendations of Rasputin.

EXTRACT C Bernard Pares, ibid.

I was bound for General Mishchenko who was in charge of an extensive section of the lines in the marshes. . . . There was a considerable staff and when I arrived they were just expecting back an ADC whom Mishchenko had sent to Petrograd to find out why all the supplies were going wrong. The officer returned during my visit; his account
5 was very simple; everything was now in the hands of Rasputin who was the tool of every kind of profiteer. The rear was by now putrefying fast.

EXTRACT D Maurice Paléologue, *An Ambassador's Memoirs*, Vol. II, entry for Friday 27 August 1915

In spite of the strict secrecy enjoined by the Emperor, his decision to take command of the army has already leaked out among the public.
  The news has produced a deplorable impression. It is objected that the Emperor has no strategic experience, he will be directly responsible for defeats the danger of which
5 is only too obvious, and lastly he has the 'evil eye'.

EXTRACT E

From: Ullstein Bilderdienst

EXTRACT F   *Letters from the Tsaritsa to the Tsar, 16 June 1915*

I always remember what our Friend says and how often we do not enough heed his
words. ... When he says not to do a thing and one does not listen one sees one's fault
always afterwards.

EXTRACT G   *Letters from the Tsaritsa to the Tsar*, 9 November 1916

Our Friend says that Sturmer can remain still some time as President of the Council of Ministers as that one does not reproach him so much, but all the row began since he became Minister of Foreign Affairs which Grigory realised in summer and told him then already that this will be your end.

EXTRACT H   Maurice Paléologue, *An Ambassador's Memoirs*, Vol. II, entry for Tuesday 12 October 1915

Has Rasputin the same power over the Emperor as over the Empress? No, there is a material difference. As regards relations between Alexandra Feodorovna and the Staretz*, she lives in a kind of hypnosis. Whatever opinion or desire he expresses she acquiesces and obeys at once. In the case of the Tsar the fascination is much less
5 passive and complete. He certainly thinks Grigory is a . . . Man of God but to a large extent he retains his liberty of judgement in dealing with him, and he never allows him the initiative. This comparative independence of mind is particularly marked when the Staretz intervenes in a political matter. . . .

*Political adviser

EXTRACT I   Richard Charques, *The Twilight of Imperial Russia*, 1958

A determining psychological factor in what followed was the religiosity of the Empress. It was the increasingly superstitious religiosity of an ailing and neurotic woman. Before she had given birth to a son and heir in the summer of 1904, Rasputin had had a predecessor of sorts, himself the latest in a line of miracle workers, in a
5 French-born mystico-medical quack named Philippe. Now after the birth of a son and heir who suffered from the incurable disease of haemophilia, the empress, her health worsening, was racked by anxiety for his life. Awkward and unhappy in public and resentful of her lack of popularity, she saw scarcely anyone outside her family or the narrowest court circle. From the first she discovered in Rasputin not only an inspired
10 vessel of Orthodoxy but also the embodiment of peasant devotion to the crown. Next came the discovery, which is supported by apparently reliable evidence from several quarters, that he could stop the Tsarevich's bleedings when the doctors had failed. It was clear to her that Rasputin could be no other than an instrument of divine Providence. As such the doors of Tsarkoe Selo were open to him.

EXTRACT J   Hugh Seton-Watson, *The Russian Empire 1801–1917*, 1967

The correspondence between the Imperial couple, published after the revolution, shows that he placed great confidence in her judgement, and that she attached importance to the views of Rasputin. Whether it is right to conclude that in Nicholas's absence the empress managed—or mismanaged—the political leadership of the Empire, and that
5 her choice of advisers was determined by Rasputin, is perhaps more doubtful. The frequent references to 'Our Friend's' approval or disapproval of individuals may prove only that the empress consulted him, not necessarily that his preferences were accepted in all cases by the Tsar, still less that the political initiative came from Rasputin. Apologists for the last emperor maintain that he made up his own mind on the merits
10 of every case, as he saw them, and argue that the legend of the power of Rasputin was created by his enemies, who deliberately exploited the minor misdeeds and discreditable character of the Siberian sectarian in order to smear the reputation of the Imperial family. The least that can be said is that the facts which were known in 1915–1916, and the further facts which became known later, lend some plausibility to the theory of
15 Rasputin's influence. At the time it was widely believed.

2 Below are a number of sources relating to the events in Amritsar, India, in 1919, and the massacre of Indian national supporters in the Jallianwala Bagh on 13 April 1919. Since the turn of the century there had been a series of reforms in India and the people believed that a greater degree of autonomy in political affairs was on the way. The British Raj were alarmed by the growth of a vociferous nationalism and were reluctant to pass over a ruling function to the Indians.

Angry flare-ups followed throughout India with the heavy hand of the police and army never very far away. In such a combustible situation which line to take, moderation or severity, was always a debatable point. General Dyer chose severity, and suffered because of this, although there were many, notably English people, both at home and in India, who claimed his fierce actions saved the day.

Questions

a Read Extracts A, B, and C.
What prevented General Dyer from taking a more moderate line of action in the Jallianwala Bagh?

b Study Extracts D, E, and F.
What evidence is there to suggest that:

(i) Dyer had already decided to take a strong line?
(ii) Dyer allowed other reasons, apart from pure security, to influence his decision?

c Study Extracts G, H, and I.
Outline the arguments put forward by those who saw Dyer as:

(i) The saviour of the Empire in India

(ii) The murderer of innocent Indians

EXTRACT A   Proclamation read out in nineteen places in Amritsar from 10.30 am onwards on 13 April 1919

No person residing in Amritsar city is permitted to leave his house after 8 pm. Any persons found in the streets after 8 pm are liable to be shot. No procession of any kind is permitted to parade the streets in the city or any part of the city or outside of it at any time.

From: A. Draper, *Amritsar*, 1981

EXTRACT B   (Signed) R. E. H. Dyer, Brigadier-General. Commanding 45th Brigade

I entered the Jallianwala Bagh by a very narrow lane which necessitated leaving my armoured cars behind. On entering I saw a dense crowd, estimated at about 5,000 (those present put it at 15,000 to 20,000); a man on a raised platform addressing the audience and making gesticulations with his hands.

5   I realized that my force was small and to hesitate might induce attack. I immediately opened fire and dispersed the mob. I estimated that between 200 and 300 of the crowd were killed. My party fired 1650 rounds.

I returned to my headquarters about 1800 hours. At 2200 hours, accompanied by a force, I visited all my pickets and marched through the city in order to make sure that
10 my order as to inhabitants not being out of their homes after 2000 hours had been obeyed. The city was absolutely quiet and not a soul was to be seen. I returned to headquarters at midnight. The inhabitants have asked permission to bury the dead in accordance with my orders. This I am allowing.

From: A. Draper, ibid.

EXTRACT C A plan of the Jallianwala Bagh, Amritsar, 1919

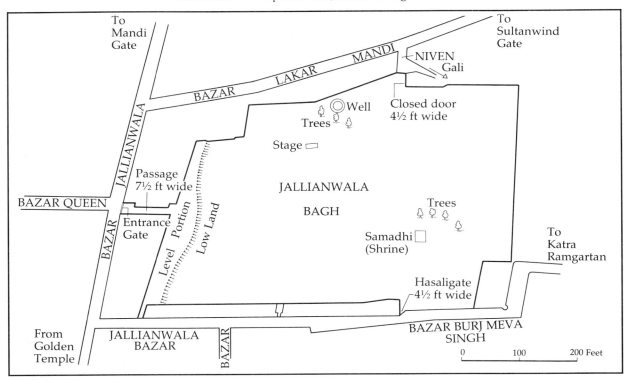

EXTRACT D General Dyer's reply to questioning by Sir Chiminlal, Hunter Commission, 1919–20

If they disobeyed my orders it showed that there was a complete defiance of law, that there was something much more serious behind it than I imagined, that therefore, these were rebels and I must not treat them with gloves on. They had come out to fight if they defied me, and I was going to give them a lesson.

From: A. Draper, ibid.

EXTRACT E General Dyer, evidence to the Hunter Commission, 1919–20

If I fired I must fire with good effect, a small amount of firing would be a criminal act of folly.

From: A. Draper, ibid.

EXTRACT F General Dyer's reply to Lord Hunter's questions asking why he did not try to disperse the crowd, Hunter Commission, 1919–20

I could not disperse them for some time, then they would come back and laugh at me, and I considered that I would be making myself a fool.

From: A. Draper, ibid.

EXTRACT G Lord Stamfordton to Chelmsford, on behalf of the King

On the one side he [Dyer] is condemned for what is regarded as heartlessness, callousness, and indifference to the value of human life, on the other side there are those who sum up their position in the words 'Dyer Saved India'.

From: A. Draper, ibid.

EXTRACT H   Memorial stone in Jallianwala Bagh

This place saturated with the blood of about 2,000 Hindu, Sikh, and Muslim patriots
who were martyred in a non-violent struggle to free India from British Domination.
General Dyer of the British Army opened fire here on unarmed people. Jallianwala
Bagh is thus an everlasting symbol of non-violent and peaceful struggle for the
5 freedom of Indian people and the gross tyranny of the British. Innocent, peaceful, and
unarmed people who were protesting against the Rowlette Acts were fired upon on
13th April, 1919. Under a resolution of the Indian National Congress this land was
purchased for Rs 565,000 for setting up a memorial to those patriots. A trust was
formed to this purpose and money collected from all over India and foreign countries.
10 When this land was purchased it was only a vacant plot and there was no garden here.
   The trust requests the people to observe the rules framed by it and thus show their
reverence to the memory of the martyrs.

From: A. Draper, ibid.

EXTRACT I   H. S. L. Polak, H. N. Brailsford, Lord Pethick-Lawrence, *Mahatma
Gandhi,* 1949

On the thirteenth a peaceful meeting was held in the enclosed garden of Jallianwala
Bagh, which had only one narrow exit. Into the trapped and tightly packed crowd of
unarmed men, General Dyer ordered his troops to fire, which they did for ten minutes
till their ammunition was exhausted. The killed, according to the official figures,
5 numbered 397 persons. The wounded, at least 1,200 persons, were left to lie where they
fell unattended. ... What especially impressed Indians, when the news of the massacre
belatedly reached England, was the feeble and divided reaction it caused there. It was
not till September that an official inquiry was held under Lord Hunter. Though it
established a damning array of facts, its conclusions were weak, and it criticised
10 General Dyer's action only in the mildest of words. He was recalled from his command
and lost his pension, but neither he nor any other officer was otherwise punished.
When Parliament debated his case, though the Government censured his actions, a
minority in the Commons and a great majority in the Lords approved of it. He was
then presented by his many admirers with a sword of honour and a purse of £20,000.

Examination advice

By now you should have gained some idea of the historical process and the
historian's work. You should be familiar with the terms **primary**, **secondary**,
reliability, **authenticity**, and **bias**, as applied to historical information. All of this
can be put to work in your historical reading, writing, and research straightaway.
There is one specific aspect of history courses where this work comes into its own
and that is in documentary source-based exercises in examinations. Section Two of
this book contains a variety of exercises on central issues in twentieth century British
and European history and uses a large number of different sources. However, before

you attempt these exercises some idea of the types of sources and questions you will encounter—as well as some words of advice—may be useful to you.

Different examination boards have different methods of using historical sources and you may encounter one, or more, of the following types in examinations.

Seen/unseen

Sources in these exercises can be **seen**, that is you have prior knowledge and familiarity with the sources and the topic from your general work, or **unseen**, when you have no such prior knowledge.

Single/multiple/gobbet

This refers to the number of extracts you are expected to deal with, ranging from one (**single**), to several long extracts (**multiple**), or a large number of smaller extracts (**gobbets**).

Primary/secondary

Some examining boards use only **primary materials**, whereas others often mix in **secondary material**, obviously providing an opportunity for the more alert candidate to make remarks about the nature of the evidence with which he has been presented.

Written/cartoon/statistical/etc.

Some boards such as London University use only written sources, and although others tend to include just written sources most, including Cambridge University, AEB, and JMB, have stated that other types of material can and will be used.

Although there is some similarity in the questions asked by boards there is also room for variation. The following points about question types should be borne in mind when attempting the exercises that follow:

- All boards include mark schemes for their questions
- Strict time limits are set on the source-based exercises
- Types of questions:

Explanation of content
Most exercises begin with a straightforward question involving reading and understanding one of the extracts.

Comparison of content
In these types of questions two or more sources have to be read and comprehended, and their basic drift and argument discussed.

Evaluating reliability and usefulness
By referring you to different extracts the examiners can test your understanding of primary and secondary sources, reliability, authenticity and bias. This can be done **internally**, by reference to other extracts provided, or, **externally**, by reference to other evidence if the document question is of the seen type.

Testing assertions/analysing
Here you may be asked to evaluate the sense, logic, and realism of a particular argument or idea in one, or more, of the sources. Again this can be done internally or externally depending on the nature of the exercise whether it is unseen or seen.

When presented with a document question you must approach it in an organised fashion because flitting through it in a vain hope of picking up the relevant information is a complete waste of time and energy. Some examiners have commented on the apparent lack of organisation and planning in candidates' answers leading to many haphazard and disorganised responses.

The first thing to do is to look at the questions very carefully making a note of the mark allocations for them because this will indicate the amount of time, energy, and hence writing needed for each of your answers. An allocation of two marks will require less of a written answer than a question carrying ten marks. This may sound very obvious but over-writing is a cardinal sin committed time and again by candidates. It also helps to underline key words in the questions: such as, 'Comment on ...', and 'Compare and contrast ....' These are specific instructions and must be followed precisely.

Most well-constructed document questions, particularly those of some length, will be organised in such a way as to lead the candidate through the printed sources one, or two, at a time until all the sources have been consulted. Hence, a first question in a typical document exercise may well have the instruction: 'Consulting Extract A only....' In such circumstances you must just refer to Extract A—in fact, you are wasting time if you do anything else. Ignore all the other extracts because they will not help you to answer the first question, and if you do refer to other extracts you will not only have wasted time but also opened yourself to the danger of trying to use information which has not been asked for in this instance. A second question in our typical example may well direct the candidate to: 'Consult Extracts B and C....' In this instance, the knowledge contained in Extract A is of no use at all and should be ignored. In this way the candidate will be led through the extracts, sometimes in order sometimes not, until the last one or two questions, when the examiner is happy that the candidate has had the opportunity to familiarise himself with all the material. At this stage more taxing questions will be asked involving assessment and evaluation.

As well as underlining key words and phrases in the extracts, making marginal comments can be very useful. This not only makes it easy to pick out relevant material to answer a specific question but it also enables a candidate to go back to a first extract at the end of a series of questions, and pick up the essence of the first extract quickly.

There are many pitfalls involved in answering document questions but the main ones are all too evident to examiners:

1 Candidates have a tendency to overwrite, especially in those questions that demand short answers. A question with an allocation of 2 marks will not require very much writing, even at 'A' level. Sometimes a couple of well-written sentences can be quite sufficient. A page and a half of the most eloquent prose, if it has missed the point—and it most certainly will have if only two marks are being awarded—cannot score more than the two marks on offer. This length of answer must be reserved for those questions that demand lengthy replies and it is by no means certain that such lengthy answers will be required, even for questions carrying 10 marks.

2 Candidates can spend far too much time on the document questions, usually to the detriment of the other sections of the paper they are sitting. The time limit, be it thirty, forty-five, or sixty minutes has been imposed because the work can, and should, be completed in the time allowed. Obviously, too much time spent on the document means that there is less time available to spend on other sections of the paper that also have to be completed to a satisfactory standard.

3   Candidates often feel that repeating what the extracts contain is an adequate answer to the questions set—it is not. Examiners look very unkindly on this practice! Merely repeating the extracts is not only copying but also it does not demonstrate the historical skills that should be displayed and, worst of all, it fails to answer a question set. Examiners are similarly uncharitable about simple paraphrasing that involves lifting whole chunks from the extracts and linking them with a few 'ands', 'buts', and 'howevers'. This practice not only leads to bad English style in answers, it clouds meaning, and again fails to answer a set question. Such answers do not demonstrate comprehension, appreciation of the subject matter, the ability to detect bias and prejudice, the skill to sift different opinions and arguments, and finally the all-important ability to communicate succinctly findings and conclusions.

A number of other minor points can also detract from the quality of candidates' answers and so result in lower marks. Always check the dates and authors of the sources used: these are part of the extracts, and can be useful in sorting out primary from secondary materials as well as helping in making an assessment of usefulness and reliability. When referring to particular sources use the extract reference letters or the author's name. Avoid stupid errors such as citing the recipient rather than the writer of a letter as the source. Do not take citations to a ridiculous length. Most boards do not expect line citations for every scrap of information, for example, '(Extract A, lines 14–17)', and many do not expect them at all. Make certain you are using the correct extracts from instructions, for example, 'Consulting Extracts A, D, and F . . . .', means just that. Do not become confused and interpose other extracts, or mis-read 'Extract E' for 'Extract F'.

Obviously you will make some of the mistakes outlined above but in doing so you will learn to be careful and systematic in your approach to documentary source-based questions. The only way to achieve this is to practise with sources. The next section contains a number of exercises covering central issues in twentieth century British and European history. Each of the exercises concentrates on a type of source (cartoon, graph, illustration, etc.); a style of presentation (single source, multiple source, etc.); or a type of question or questions. Each of the exercises has a mark scheme, a time allocation, and there are a limited number of specimen answers. Exercises 1 and 3 in the British and European Sections are provided with specimen answers which are not designed to be models but merely full responses to the questions posed, demonstrating the length, complexity, and possible structure of potential answers.

Section Two

This section has three parts. The first two parts contain exercises based on twentieth century British and European examples respectively.

Each exercise is preceded by a short and general introduction to the topic concerned. This is designed to do no more than set the exercise in context and varies from exercise to exercise, sometimes outlining the events that led to a particular episode; at other times concentrating on the events themselves, and occasionally examining the recent historiography of particular topics.

Each introduction is followed by a brief and selective bibliography which gives some idea of the range of texts available in each of the subject areas. The length and level of the texts vary, and where appropriate each bibliography has been divided into *Section A*, containing the more short, general, and 'A' level texts, including pamphlets, and *Section B* containing longer, more demanding, and specialised texts. Consequently, both the student attempting a broader general syllabus and the one tackling a narrower specialised paper will be catered for in these bibliographies. In some cases suitable books are limited and to a certain extent they select themselves because very little else is available, but for most of the exercises the difficulty has been in keeping the number of books cited to a manageable size.

Examples of relevant essay questions taken from recent papers of the examining boards follow the bibliographies. A range of questions, from the straightforward to the difficult, has been selected. A few of the topics dealt with in the exercises are quite specialised and appear on papers intermittently, while most never seem to be omitted. In order to find an adequate range of questions both General Papers and Special Subject Papers have been used. The key below explains the source of each of the essay questions. The questions at the end of each topic develop in degree of difficulty from first to last. However, degree of difficulty may reflect the complexity of the question and answer; the amount of material to be dealt with at any one time, and, the amount of writing required.

The third part of this section contains 'gobbets', which are, as explained in Section One, short snippets of information. Again, twentieth century British and European examples are included. Sometimes you may be presented with a number of gobbets, and asked to select three or four and comment on them. This undirected type of exercise can be a little daunting. On pages 80–81 you will find a 'checklist' to help you plan an approach to these.

Key

AEB	Associated Examining Board
JMB	Joint Matriculation Board
ODLE	Oxford Delegacy of Local Examinations
OCSEB	Oxford and Cambridge Schools Examinations Board
UCLES	University of Cambridge Local Examinations Syndicate
UL	University of London
Sp. Sub.	Example taken from a Special Subject Paper. All others are taken from General Outline Papers
Specimen	Taken from a Specimen Paper
'81 etc.	The year the essay appeared in the examination.

Anglo-German naval rivalry

The rivalry which existed between Germany and Great Britain at the end of the nineteenth century and beginning of the twentieth century was concentrated on trade, colonies, and naval power. The latter was quite intense because a large navy was not only relevant for national defence but also a very visible manifestation of national power and strength. This Anglo-German naval rivalry has received considerable attention since 1914, because of its obvious relationship to the growth of militarism which may have been a contributory factor to the outbreak of the First World War.

Britain's navy protected her shores, trade, markets, and sources of raw materials, and enabled her to monitor and control her far-flung Empire. Any nation with pretensions to world power status, and even dominance, would need a similar naval capacity.

As Germany grew in status and strength in the last quarter of the nineteenth century so did her desire for a navy to protect and promote her world interests. At first it seemed unlikely that Germany would out-strip Britain in naval terms, and most strategists believed that this might not be necessary. Britain's dominance was based on the fact that she had more ships than her closest rivals. Germany's entry into the naval race complicated the issue. If, as most Germans believed, the next war was to be between Britain on the one hand and France and Russia on the other, then Germany might well find herself the leading naval power after such a conflict. Hence, it was only necessary for Germany to produce ships at a rate that allowed her to keep Britain in her sights, and, Germany was aided considerably by the developments in ship design and building made at this stage. In 1906, HMS *Dreadnought* revolutionised the naval world. It was bigger, quicker, and more powerful than any other class of ship that had gone before. Almost overnight, many previously useful vessels were obsolete and Germany had a golden opportunity to close the gap on Britain. Germany tried, but did not succeed in matching Britain 'Dreadnought for Dreadnought'. Britain was spending vast amounts of money on building programmes, and the shipyards were highly productive. Certainly, Britain enjoyed an advantage over Germany in 1914 and benefited from the strength of her navy, especially in the blockade of Germany. Her mastery of the seas seemed as complete in 1914 as it had been one hundred years before. The document exercise below outlines the reasons behind the rivalry and highlights the intensity of the struggle between Germany and Britain in the naval arms race.

Select Bibliography

Section A

H. Kurtz, *The Second Reich: Kaiser Wilhelm II and his Germany*, Macdonald (1970)

J. Telford, *British Foreign Policy 1870–1914*, Blackie (1978)

Section B

M. Balfour, *The Kaiser and His Times*, Pelican (1975)

P. M. Kennedy, *The Rise of Anglo-German Antagonism, 1860–1914*, Allen & Unwin (1982)

E. L. Woodward, *Great Britain and the German Navy*, Frank Cass (1968)

Essays

a Account for the growing hostility between Britain and Germany in the period 1890–1914. (ODLE 81)

b By what stages and for what reasons did Britain move into a hostile relationship with Germany in the period 1900–14? (UL 83)

c Discuss the major factors which affected the relations between Britain and Germany in the period 1898 to 1914. (JMB 84)

Exercise One: Unseen

Multiple extract style.   20 marks.   Time allowed: 50 minutes

EXTRACT A   Memorandum of the OberKommando of the German Navy, June 1894

A state which has oceanic or—an equivalent term— world interests must be able to uphold them and make its power felt beyond its own territorial matters. National world commerce, world industry, and to a certain extent fishing on the high seas, world inter- course and colonies are impossible without a fleet capable of taking the offensive. The conflicts of interests between nations, the lack of confidence felt by capital and the business world will either destroy these expressions of the vitality of a state or prevent them from taking form, if they are not supported by national power on the seas, and therefore beyond our own waters. Herein lies by far the most important purpose of the fleet.

From: E. L. Woodward, Great Britain and the German Navy, 1964

EXTRACT B *Punch, 3 August 1889*

VISITING GRANDMAMMA.

GRANDMA' VICTORIA. "NOW, WILLIE DEAR, YOU'VE PLENTY OF *SOLDIERS* AT HOME; LOOK AT THESE PRETTY *SHIPS*,—I'M SURE YOU'LL BE PLEASED WITH *THEM*!"

EXTRACT D *Punch, 24 March 1909*

COPYRIGHT EXPIRES.

GERMAN TAR." 'WE DON'T WANT TO FIGHT, BUT, BY JINGO, IF WE DO,
WE'VE GOT THE SHIPS, WE'VE GOT THE MEN, WE'VE GOT THE MONEY TOO.' "
JOHN BULL. "I SAY, THAT'S *MY* OLD SONG."
GERMAN TAR. "WELL, IT'S MINE NOW."

EXTRACT C

Uncle Edward (to William), 'Your little marine masterpiece is too ambitious; keep it as a study.'

From: BBC Hulton Picture Library

EXTRACT E

Table 1 Relative strengths of Germany and Britain in Battleships and Dreadnoughts 1907–11

| Year | Battleships | | | | Dreadnoughts | | | |
| | Less than 15 yrs | | Under construction | | Completed | | Under construction | |
	GB	G	GB	G	GB	G	GB	G
1907	47	21	5	8	1	0	3	4
1908	40	21	8	9	1	0	6	7
1909	43	22	6	10	2	0	6	10
1910	45	23	9	8	5	2	9	8
1911	43	24	10	9	8	4	10	9

From: E. L. Woodward, ibid.

EXTRACT F W. A. Von Stumm, 8 September 1908

I am inclined to think, although I appear to be stating a paradox, that the British anxiety about the development of our fleet may facilitate the conclusion of an agreement. The ... nervousness with which all England
5 watches the growth of our forces at sea, the heavy financial burdens imposed by the attempt to be twice as strong as ourselves, the difficulties ... in the way of immobilising almost the whole of the British Fleet in the North Sea, all these considerations seem to me to show
10 that our naval policy gives us a valuable trump-card in relation to England.

From: E. L. Woodward, ibid.

EXTRACT G Sir Edward Grey, Speech in the House of Commons, 29 March 1909

There is no comparison between the importance of the German navy to Germany, and the importance of our navy to us. Our navy is to us what their army is to them. To have a strong navy would increase their
5 prestige, their diplomatic influence, their power of protecting their commerce, but as regards us—it is not a matter of life and death to them that as it is to us. No superiority of the British navy over the German navy could ever put us in a position to affect the inde-
10 pendence or integrity of Germany, because our army is not maintained on a scale which, unaided, could do anything on German territory. But if the German navy were superior to ours, they, maintaining the army which they do, for us it would not be a question of defeat.
15 Our independence, our very existence would be at stake.

From: E. L. Woodward, ibid.

Questions

a   Using only Extract A, give reasons for Germany's desire to have a navy. *(4)*

b   (i)   What other reasons for Germany's desire for a larger navy are suggested in cartoon Extracts B and C? *(3)*

(ii)   By referring to Extract E, can you detect any bias in Extract D? *(4)*

c   How far are Von Stumm's ideas in Extract F substantiated by the views and evidence contained in Extracts E and G? *(9)*

(20 marks)

Specimen answers are on p. 59.

Liberal Party victory, 1906 election

When Henry Campbell-Bannerman was summoned by the King on 4 December 1905, he realised that the first Liberal government in twenty years would be formed as a direct result of the Conservative and Unionist parties' internal disagreements. The so-called 'Khaki' election in 1900 had given the Conservatives a majority of about 130 which was still into three figures by 1905. However, the need for a Liberal government was a result of the intense debate that was going on in Conservative circles, as well as throughout the nation, on the question of Joseph Chamberlain's proposals for tariff reform, or Imperial Preference. Chamberlain believed that Imperial Defence was the Empire's concern and that each colony ought to contribute to its own protection, and in order to tie the Empire closer together, a common trading policy based on Protection would serve the purpose and the revenue raised would provide for social reform in Britain. Unfortunately, such a scheme would also raise the price of many basic raw materials from other areas, and more importantly would increase the cost of foods imported into Britain.

In addition, the Conservatives had been criticized for many of their actions in government since 1900. The undistinguished Boer War victory revealed fundamental defence and military problems. The 1902 Education Act had enraged Non-Conformists whose rate payments would be used to finance both Church of England and Catholic schools and the Licensing Act annoyed Temperance supporters who believed landlords incited drunkenness by selling alcohol and so should not be compensated for their loss of licences. The working man had also been offended by the Lords' judgement on the Taff Vale Case, and many felt disenchanted with Conservative rule. In the election contest that followed Campbell-Bannerman's summons to the palace in 1905, it was hardly surprising that the Conservatives would lose seats. What was astonishing was the scale of their defeat, gaining only 157 seats to the Liberals 400. Obviously the policies pursued by the Conservatives accounted for much of the Liberal victory, but other points need to be mentioned: for instance, the way the election became an expression of the feelings of the poor against the rich, and how the so-called 'compact' with the Unionists forced Balfour to keep faith with Chamberlain throughout the tariff issue. Moreover, Balfour failed to keep a united front and many of his cabinet colleagues spoke out against government policies. Therefore, the victory in 1906 was effectively given away by the Conservatives to the Liberals. The document exercise below attempts to highlight the main issues during the election contest which led on to the Liberal landslide of 1906.

Select Bibliography

Section A

A. O'Day (ed.), *The Edwardian Age: Conflict and Stability, 1900–1914*, Macmillan (1979)

E. J. Feuchtwanger, *Democracy and Europe: Britain 1865–1914*, Edward Arnold (1985)

D. Read, *Edwardian England, 1901–1915: Society and Politics*, Harrap (1972)

Section B

M. Egremont, *Balfour: A Life of Arthur James Balfour*, Collins (1980)

J. Enoch Powell, *Joseph Chamberlain*, Thames and Hudson (1977)

A. K. Russell, *Liberal Landslide: The General Election of 1906*, David & Charles Archon (1973)

Essays

a How far can the defeat of the Conservatives in 1906 be attributed to Joseph Chamberlain's tariff reform campaign? (ODLE 82)

b 'It was not the Liberals who won, but the Conservatives who lost the General Election of 1906'. Discuss. (UL 83)

c 'Balfour must share the responsibility with Chamberlain for the overwhelming Conservative defeat in the 1906 election'. Comment on this view. (JMB 85)

Exercise Two: Unseen

Multiple extract style.   20 marks.   Time allowed: 40 minutes

EXTRACT A   *Quarterly Review*, April 1906

It is true that many grievances co-operated to make the Unionist Party unpopular [but] it is also true that most of these different grievances had some common elements so that they appeared to the electorate like the
5 various counts at a single indictment rather than a number of distinct charges. Thus the attack on Chinese Labour, on Protection, and on the Taff Vale judgement, all formed part of an accusation of plutocratic conspiracy. Even the Education Act was represented as a
10 victory for privilege, and so fell in with the general charge that the Unionists were the party of the rich and selfish who were ready to degrade the British Empire in South Africa by gathering gold through the labour of slaves, to build up a system of monopoly by taxing the
15 food of the poor, to keep the public schools of the nation as a preserve for their own friends and to put the

20 workmen under the heel of the Capitalist by overthrowing the trade unions. The issue thus seemed to be Rich versus Poor ... [and] it was to no purpose that the Unionist candidates argued one point or another. There was no escaping the general impression ... the Unionist Party was branded as the plutocratic party; and if the particular candidate were not himself one of their conspirators, he was their dupe.

EXTRACT B   Profile of Liberal Election Addresses, showing percentage of candidates mentioning major issues, 1906

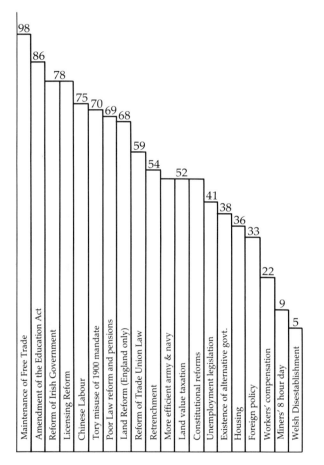

Bar value	Issue
98	Maintenance of Free Trade
86	Amendment of the Education Act
78	Reform of Irish Government
75	Licensing Reform
70	Chinese Labour
69	Tory misuse of 1900 mandate
68	Poor Law reform and pensions
59	Land Reform (England only)
54	Reform of Trade Union Law
52	Retrenchment
41	More efficient army & navy
38	Land value taxation
36	Constitutional reforms
33	Unemployment legislation
22	Existence of alternative govt.
9	Housing
5	Foreign policy

From: A. K. Russell, *Liberal Landslide: the General Election of 1906*, 1973

EXTRACT C   *Manchester Guardian*, 15 January 1906

A candidate had only to be a Free Trader to get in, whether he was known or unknown, semi-Unionist or thorough Home Ruler, Protestant or Roman Catholic, entertaining or dull. He had only to be a Protectionist
5 to lose all chance of getting in though he spoke with the tongues of men and angels, though he was a good employer to many electors, or had led the House of Commons or fought in the Crimea.

42

EXTRACT D   'Real Wage' Index, 1890–1913 (1890–99 = 100)

Year	Wood	Bowley	Phelps Brown and Browne	Kuczynski
1890	99	96	96	100
1891	103	95	96	98
1892	93	95	95	95
1893	94	97	96	95
1894	96	101	101	97
1895	99	103	103	100
1896	103	103	103	104
1897	103	101	103	103
1898	103	102	101	103
1899	107	107	106	107
1900	108	106	104	105
1901	106	105	105	111
1902	103	104	103	102
1903		102	102	100
1904		100	101	98
1905		100	100	99
1906		101	103	102
1907		104	105	102
1908		104	106	97
1909		103	104	95
1910		101	104	98
1911		100	102	99
1912		100	102	97
1913		100	101	100

EXTRACT E   Number of unopposed returns, Unionist and Liberal, 1885–1906 (England, Scotland, and Wales)

Year	Total no. of seats	Total no. of unopposed returns	No. of Unionist returns unopposed	No. of Liberal returns unopposed (inc. LRC)
1885	567	26	7	19
1886	567	153	114	39
1892	567	51	33	18
1895	567	135	123	12
1900	567	176	153	23
1906	567	37	5	32

From: A. K. Russell, ibid.

Questions

a (i) Consult Extract A. What issues does the *Quarterly Review* pin-point as being important in the election? *(6)*

(ii) How far does Extract B bear out the points raised by Extract A and what conclusion can you draw about the Liberal party's electioneering tactics? *(5)*

b Is the assessment of the *Manchester Guardian* in Extract C a reasonable one in the light of the evidence presented in Extracts A and B? *(2)*

c How might the 'Rich versus the Poor' (Extract A, lines 18–19) have been a real issue in the election? Use Extract D. *(4)*

d What other reason for the Liberals' victory is revealed in Extract E? *(3)*

(20 marks)

Ireland, 1912–14

Virtually from its inception, the Act of Union was a target for Irish patriots who realised that it would have to be repealed if Ireland was ever to achieve independence. Despite their efforts, by the last quarter of the nineteenth century the Irish still awaited an English Government committed to such a measure. The Liberals seemed the most likely party to pursue a policy of Home Rule for Ireland. However, William Gladstone, the Liberal Prime Minister, failed to achieve Home Rule both in 1886 and 1893. Perhaps the greatest stumbling block was the division that existed in Ireland between Protestant and Catholic, agriculture and industry, and North and South. The northern Province of Ulster saw its interests best served by a continuation of the Union with England. This would ensure a greater growth for its industry and more protection for its mainly Protestant population. The rest of Ireland could see no point in gaining an independence that divided the nation and demanded that Ulster should not be granted any special treatment. The depth of feeling and passion aroused by the issue was great. It was enough to ensure that the Nationalists of the South and the Unionists of the North saw their best interests as being diametrically opposed to each other. However, the Unionists, with strong English support (especially from the House of Lords) seemed safe because any Bills for Home Rule proposed by whatever government could be killed-off in the Lords.

This stone-walling seemed set to continue for ever, but the situation suddenly changed when Asquith's Liberal Government took on the House of Lords over the issue of Lloyd George's budget in 1909. The struggle that ensued led directly to the passing of the Parliament Act in 1911 which curtailed the Lord's powers to block legislation. In future, bills that had passed the Commons three times in the space of two years would become law and this opened the door for Home Rule. A Third Home Rule Bill was proposed in 1912 with every likelihood of success in two years. The Unionists immediately gathered their forces under the leadership of Sir Edward Carson and civil war became a real possibility. The Unionists would not bow to the Irish majority. Asquith's government desperately sought to find compromises and tried to make the Bill more palatable to the Unionists by a partial exclusion amendment for Ulster for a period of six years. The compromise suggested pleased no one and the government was saved further embarrassment when the First World War broke out in the summer of 1914. The Irish Nationalists suggested a suspension of Home Rule for the duration of hostilities, although more violent events in 1916 were to overtake the country well before Parliament could discuss the issue of Home Rule again.

Select Bibliography

Section A

J. C. Beckett, *The Making of Modern Ireland, 1603–1923*, Faber (1981)

P. Buckland, *Irish Unionism, 1885–1922*, Historical Association (1973)

M. J. Winstanley, *Ireland and the Land Question, 1800–1922*, Methuen (1984)

Section B

P. Buckland, *Irish Unionism*, Volumes I and II, Gill Macmillan (1972 and 1973)

N. Mansergh, *The Irish Question, 1840–1921*, Allen & Unwin (1965)

Essays

a Why was Irish Home Rule not achieved in the period 1874–1914? (UCLES 83)

b 'By 1914 the Irish Land Problem was well on the way towards being solved but the problem of Ulster and the growth of Republicanism remained a stumbling block to a solution of the Irish Question.' Comment on this statement. (JMB 81)

c 'The Ulster Question which blew up only when Home Rule became a real possibility ruined all hopes of a peaceful settlement of the Home Rule controversy.' Examine the truth of this statement. (UL 84)

Exercise Three: Seen

Multiple extract style.   20 marks.   Time allowed: 45 minutes

EXTRACT A   Edward Carson and the Ulster Covenant signed in Belfast, reported in *The Times*, 19 September 1912

Being convinced in our consciences that Home Rule would be disastrous to the material well being of Ulster as well as the whole of Ireland, and perilous to the unity of the Empire, we, whose names are underwritten,
5 men of Ulster, loyal subjects of his gracious Majesty George V, humbly relying on God whom our fathers in days of stress and trial confidently trusted, do hereby pledge ourselves in solemn covenant throughout this our time of threatened calamity to stand by one another
10 in defending for ourselves and for our children our cherished position of equal citizenship in the United Kingdom and in using all means which may be found necessary to defeat this present conspiracy to set up a Home Rule Parliament in Ireland. And in the event of
15 such a Parliament being forced on us we further solemnly mutually pledge ourselves to refuse to recognise its authority. In sure confidence that God will defend the right we hereto subscribe our names . . . God Save the King.

EXTRACT B   Rudyard Kipling, 'Ulster 1912'

> We know the war prepared
> On every peaceful home,
> We know the hells declared
> For such as serve not Rome—
> 5 The Terror, threats, and dread
> In market, hearth, and field—
> We know, when all is said,
> We perish if we yield.

> What answer from the North?
> 10 One Law, one Land, one Throne,
> If England drives us forth
> We shall not fall alone.

EXTRACT C   Edward Carson, *Parliamentary Debates*, 5/lviii/176–177, 11 February 1914

Believe me, whatever way you settle the Irish Question, there are only two ways to deal with Ulster. It is for statesmen to say which is the best and right one. She is not part of the community which can be bought. She
5 will not allow herself to be sold. You must therefore either coerce her if you go on, or you must, in the long run, by showing that good government can come under the Home Rule Bill, try to win her over to the case of the rest of Ireland. You can probably coerce her—
10 though I doubt it. If you do, what will be the disastrous consequence not only to Ulster, but to this country and the Empire?

EXTRACT D   Notes made by Maj-Gen. Sir Henry Wilson on a conversation with Bonar Law, A. P. Ryan, *Mutiny on the Curragh*, 1956

. . . that there was much talk in the army, and that if we were ordered to coerce Ulster there would be wholesale defections. It has been suggested to him (Bonar Law) that 40 per cent of officers and men would leave the
5 army. Personally I put the pc. much lower, but still very serious. I then told him of Cecil's idea that Carson should pledge the Ulster troops to fight for England if she were at war. I pointed out that a move like this would render the employment of troops against Ulster
10 more impossible than ever . . . .

Asquith was going to approach B.L. with a proposal to exclude the four Northern counties. This, of course, wrecks the present Bill and puts B.L. into an awkward position, as Ulster won't agree; and then Asquith can
15 claim intolerance. On the other hand, Asquith is in a much tighter place, because Johnny Redmond and Devlin can't agree to the exclusion of Ulster. The thing to do, therefore, is to make Redmond wreck the proposal. . . .

Questions

a What does Carson see as the two biggest drawbacks to Home Rule in Extract A?   *(1)*

b How does Kipling portray the religious side of Ulster defiance in Extract B?   *(2)*

c How far does Kipling's poem reflect the ideas, fears, and plans put forward by Carson and the Ulstermen in 1912?   *(5)*

d What two solutions does Carson offer Westminster in Extract C? *(2)*

e Using Extract D explain why coercion of Ulster was out of the question in 1914. *(2)*

f (i) What was the compromise solution reached on Home Rule in 1914? *(4)*

(ii) How would Asquith's proposal (Extract D, line 13) 'wreck the present bill'? *(2)*

(iii) How was Home Rule made a dead letter by the summer of 1914? *(2)*

(20 marks)

Specimen answers are on pp. 59–60.

Female emancipation

The general exclusion of women from the three great nineteenth century Parliamentary Reform Acts of 1832, 1867, and 1884 was a reflection of the attitude to the role of women at that time. The line between the sexes was very firmly drawn, with marriage, child-bearing, and domesticity being the designated pattern for all women to follow. Such entrenched attitudes have still not been eradicated but in the nineteenth century and early twentieth century they were deeply engraved.

However, with changes in British society, particularly the greater availability of education for females and some recognition of legal rights, the more well-to-do females were not as constrained as their less fortunate counterparts. Nevertheless, the arguments put forward for not allowing greater female participation in the political sphere still concentrated on the belief that the 'weaker sex' were mentally and physically inferior. Most men were convinced that women were incapable of coping with the demanding tasks of the male world and were far safer at home. Part of the lack of success in changing these attitudes was that many *women* accepted them as true and were perfectly willing to accept a position secondary to that of men. But, the continuing growth of education and the pioneering work of many leading female figures such as Miss Beale, Miss Buss, Dr Stopes, Mrs Pankhurst and the Pankhurst daughters slowly presented a picture of the future in which women would be recognised as individuals in their own right. Stating this as true was relatively easy but providing opportunities for women to prove that they were the equal of men in all fields of human endeavour was very difficult. It is interesting to note that the final extensions of the franchise to all women, on a national rather than local level, were to follow on the heels of the end of the First World War relatively quickly. By 1929 all women would have the vote and although the efforts of the Suffragettes were important, it was the role played by the nation's women during the years 1914 to 1918 that really paved the way for change. The activities of millions of women on the Home Front and for the war effort, while men were away fighting in the trenches, were the most potent and clear demonstration of women's ability to do the same jobs as men. This eventually brought its reward in the political arena with the extension of the suffrage, by stages, to all women. The document exercise that follows examines the conflict over women's role in society before the outbreak of the First World War.

Select Bibliography

Section A

A. O'Day (ed.), *The Edwardian Age*, Macmillan (1979)

M. Pugh, *Women's Suffrage in Britain, 1867–1928*, Historical Association (1980)

D. Read, *Edwardian England, 1901–1915: Society and Politics*, Harrap (1972)

Section B

A. Raeburn, *The Militant Suffragettes*, David & Charles (1976)

R. Strachey, *The Cause: A Short History of the Women's Movement*, first published 1928, Virago (1978)

Essays

a Discuss the progress made by 1914 towards emancipation for women. (JMB 82)

b To what extent have women's achievements since 1928 justified the efforts and aspirations of the Suffragettes? (UCLES 83)

c Assess the importance of developments during the First World War in advancing the opportunities for women in Britain. (AEB 83)

Exercise Four: Unseen

Multiple extract style.   20 marks.   Time allowed: 45 minutes

EXTRACT A   Mr Grant, *Parliamentary Papers*, 5 May 1913

I have no hesitation myself in voting against the principle of giving the vote to women . . . . It is difficult to put arguments before hon. Members who believe in sex equality. The real point at issue is whether women
5 have the same capacity for government as men, and whether they are possessed of the qualifications for ruling and government. We have heard many arguments as to why women should have votes; we are told there are women with plenty of money who probably
10 employ men or many men who have the vote and we are asked 'Why should not they have votes also?' We are asked, 'Is not the intellect of women as acute as the intellect of men?'. That is put to us with somewhat irritating consistency . . . in passing such a bill as this we
15 shall be taking a step which will lead to the ultimate enfranchisement of women and giving the mastery and control of the government of this country into female hands . . . it is surely undemocratic to enable a minority of women who are in favour of the vote to force the
20 vote upon an unwilling majority. Some hon. Members believe that there is a majority of women in favour of the vote but I think the reverse is the case. I cannot conceive a greater abuse of the power of this House than to force female government upon an unwilling
25 majority in this country. . . . We are controlled and worried enough by women at the present time and I have heard no reason given why we should alter this present state of affairs. A clever woman said to me the other day, 'if at the most critical period of a woman's
30 life she had not got the sense to say "no" to the man who proposes to her, how can you expect her to have the sense to vote on a great Imperial Question?'. I would urge all hon. Members to consider seriously before they vote for this measure.

EXTRACT B   Marie Corelli, *Woman or Suffragette*, 1907

'Votes for Women'! is the shrill cry of a number of apparently discontented ladies who somehow seem to have missed the best of life. And it is well-nigh useless to re-iterate the plain, trite truth that Woman was and is
5 destined to make voters rather than to be one of them. . . .
    It cannot, of course, be denied that women have suffered, and still are destined to suffer, great injustice at the hands of men. But again, that is the result of the
10 way in which mothers have reared their sons and still

continue to rear them. . . . Women have quite as good brains as men,—they can become great artists, great writers, great scientists,—that is, if they choose to practise the self-denial and endure the hardships which
15 are the necessary accompaniments to these careers— they might even become great musicians, if with depth of sentiment, they could also obtain self-control . . . .

EXTRACT C   Lord Henry Cavendish-Bentinck, *Parliamentary Papers*, 5 May 1913

I cannot help thinking that a revolution has also taken place amongst us of late years. The industrial development of this country has transformed the status of women. It is really, I think, idle now to talk of the
5 sacredness of the home when modern industry, mills, factories, workshops, offices, and warehouses, are everywhere claiming thousands and thousands of young men and young women. Side by side with this important development there is also a movement, the
10 strength and force of which we cannot deny. The whole of the working world is weary of the past of being exploited by the economists and treated as machines and are everywhere, with increasing persistence, demanding opportunities for intellectual improvement
15 for themselves and their children, and also for better homes and new, cleaner, and better surroundings. They have found out and are finding out that it is within their power by the expression of their collective will as expressed in Parliament to obtain these benefits for
20 themselves. So it seems to me the movement is a movement in which women are certainly fitted to take part. I for one do not for a moment allow that women are so markedly inferior to the male sex as to be incapable of taking this part.

EXTRACT D   W. L. Blease, *The Emancipation of English Women*, 1910

To the early Suffragists and to their successors the Parliamentary franchise has thus been more than a mere means of influencing Government. It has always appeared as a symbol of social worth. So long as it is
5 enjoyed by men, and by them denied to women , so long must women be in a state of subjection and exposed to innumerable wrongs which are not directly connected with votes. The captain is not more clearly the superior of the soldier whom he commands than is
10 the man that of the woman whose position in society he prescribes. It is useless to declaim upon the equal or superior worth of women, so long as men exercise their power to exclude them from any sphere of activity which they may desire to enter. It is useless, indeed, to
15 declare that they are willing to admit women into everything except politics. The very declaration, even if

it were true, is an assertion of their power and their
intention to direct the lives of women not according to
the wishes of women themselves, but according to their
20 own. The exclusion from national politics would
outweigh all the other privileges. Mere inability to
obtain degrees at Cambridge, or to enter the legal
profession, or to serve on juries, would be slight things
in comparison. But in a country where politics bulk so
25 largely as in England, disfranchisement stamps and
brands the disfranchised with an indelible mark of
inferiority. The person who, being an adult, is not fit to
take part in English politics, will inevitably encounter all
the consequences of subjection in education, in pro-
30 fessional and industrial employments, and in social
intercourse , whenever he or she has to do with those
who are invested with all the dignity of citizenship. The
disfranchisement of women is thus intimately connected
not only with their remaining political and legal
35 disabilities, but also with their inferior training , their
narrower outlook upon life and their consequent
defects of character, with their inadequate rewards for
services, and with their purely sexual grievances of
marital subjection and prostitution.

Questions

a   Read Extract A. What reasons does Grant put forward
to doubt the sense of giving women the vote? What is
his ultimate fear and why does he have this fear?   *(5)*

b   How far does Marie Corelli, in Extract B, agree with
Grant's views about women's unsuitability for the
franchise?   *(4)*

c   What arguments are mentioned in Extract A and put
forward in Extract C in favour of female suffrage?   *(6)*

d   How does Extract D

  (i)   Widen the arguments about female suffrage into a
general social question?   *(3)*

  (ii)   Ultimately alight upon the vote as the key issue for
women?   *(2)*

(20 marks)

General Strike, 1926

The willingness of trade unionists to fight for their country
in 1914 was gratifying for the government, especially after
the fraught years before the outbreak of the war. This pre-
war period had seen unions and governments at logger-
heads over the Taff Vale Case, the Osborne Judgment, and
the Docks Strikes of 1911 and 1912. There was also the
threat of concerted union action by the Trade Union
Movement, relying on the considerable disruptive strength
of the so-called 'Triple Alliance' of miners, railwaymen, and
transport workers who included in their number the seamen
and dockers. Any such hopes for union cooperation were
postponed during the war years and even after 1918 the
harsh realities of the post-war world sapped much of the
unions' resolve.

However, government decontrol of the mines in 1921 in
the face of heavy losses left the owners with the task of
reducing wages to save money. The miners refused to
accept any reductions and were locked out. Attempts to re-
invoke the Triple Alliance failed on 'Black Friday' (15 April)
and the miners were forced to return to work for less
money. This situation continued until 1924 when wages

were increased, but a sharp downturn in trade forced the
owners to reduce wages once again in 1925.

The miners appealed to the Unions' General Council, and
this time, perhaps prompted by guilt, the Union movement
responded. The government acted quickly and offered a
subsidy to cover miners' lost wages, it set up the Samuel
Commission, and made contingency plans to counter
further troubles. These were not far away. Part of the
Samuel Commission's recommendations was a reduction in
wages. This led by stages to the General Strike of 1926.
Supporting the miners' cry of, 'Not a penny off the pay, not
a minute on the day', there was a surprising degree of
unanimity of action by workers in the first days of the strike.
However, the government was well prepared with its
organisation for the maintenance of supplies, recruitment of
volunteers, propaganda, and, as a last resort, the army.
Nevertheless, the potential for political chaos was worrying
for the government and the trade union movement. It was
this fear and the government's opposition that persuaded
the General Council to accept a peace plan, but unfortunately they did so without miners' representatives being

consulted. The general return to work was ordered for 12 May and it was left to the miners to fight on alone. Not only did the Union movement have to accept defeat but it suffered major losses of members and money, and more importantly, the government passed the Trades Disputes Act in 1927 which severely limited future national exhibitions of workers' solidarity. The document exercise that follows traces the events of 1926 and examines attitudes towards the General Strike.

Select Bibliography

Section A

P. Adelman, *The Rise of the Labour Party, 1880–1945*, Seminar Studies in History, Longman (1972)

J. Lovell, *British Trade Unions, 1875–1933*, Macmillan (1977)

M. Morris, *The British General Strike, 1926*, Historical Association (1973)

A. J. P. Taylor, *English History, 1914–1945*, Oxford University Press (1965)

Section B

R. I. Hills, *The General Strike in York*, Borthwick Papers, St Anthony's Press, York (1980)

H. Pelling, *A History of British Trade Unionism*, Penguin (1973)

J. Symons, *The General Strike*, Cresset Press (1957)

Essays

a How serious a setback for the Labour Movement was the failure of the General Strike of 1926? (UL 84)

b Why did the fortunes of the British coalmining industry dominate the industrial scene in Britain between 1919 and 1927? (JMB 83)

c Discuss the view that 'the General Strike will be seen as one of the most significant landmarks in the History of the working-class' (Beatrice Webb 1926). (UCLES 82)

Exercise Five: Unseen

Multiple extract style.   20 marks.   Time allowed: 40 minutes

EXTRACT A   Presidential Address, Trades Union Congress, *Annual Report*, 1926

The stoppage of the principal transport and other industries of this country in May last has been termed a general strike, a term which has been deliberately misused by our adversaries to justify the false assertion
5 that its purpose was to hold up the life of the country ... It will be fatal to the welfare of this country ... if that great and spontaneous demonstration of working-class solidarity ... so inspiring as a revelation of the true spirit of Trade Union brotherhood, is regarded as

the outcome of a sort of evil conspiracy of a few
10 agitators ...

On a previous occasion when the workers showed the same impressive unanimity in making common cause, when from field and factory, workshop and mine
15 they poured into the trenches in France and Flanders ... their action evoked a different response from other classes ...

The supreme lesson of the national strike is the clear evidence it adduced as showing that the Trade Union
20 Movement retains the belief in the essential rightness of democratic methods. All that could be done in the way of provocation by agents of the Government to goad our people into acts of violence and disorder, was resorted to. The ostentatious display of military force
25 ... the flaming manifestoes of Mr Winston Churchill in the government strike organ ... none of it caused our people to turn aside from the declared objective and limited purpose of the stoppage. It was not the unions but the Government which endeavoured to convert an
30 industrial struggle into political conflict, and sought to make party capital out of it. Nothing but the restraint of our members prevented the agents of the Government fomenting a revolutionary temper and plunging the country into ... civil war ...

EXTRACT B   *Punch*, 12 May 1926

UNDER WHICH FLAG?
JOHN BULL, "ONE OF THESE TWO FLAGS HAS GOT TO COME DOWN—
AND IT WON'T BE MINE."

EXTRACT C
*Lansbury's
Labour Weekly*, 22
May 1926

In answer to the "British Gazette"

UNDER WHICH FLAG?

From: The British
Library

EXTRACT D

Year	Total no. of members of trade unions (000s)	Working days lost (000s)	Year	Total no. of members of trade unions (000s)	Working days lost (000s)
1906	1,997	3,019	1924	5,429	8,424
1907	2,210	2,148	1925	5,544	7,952
1908	2,513	10,785	1926	5,506	162,233
1909	2,485	2,687	1927	5,219	1,174
1910	2,477	9,867	1928	4,919	1,388
1911	2,565	10,155	1929	4,866	8,287
1912	3,139	40,890	1930	4,858	4,399
1913	3,416	9,804	1931	4,842	6,983
1914	4,135	9,878	1932	4,642	6,488
1915	4,145	2,953	1933	4,444	1,072
1916	4,359	2,446	1934	4,392	959
1917	4,644	5,647	1935	4,590	1,955
1918	5,499	5,875	1936	4,867	1,829
1919	6,533	34,969	1937	5,295	3,413
1920	7,926	26,568	1938	5,842	1,334
1921	8,348	85,872	1939	6,053	1,356
1922	6,633	19,850	1940	6,298	940
1923	5,625	10,672			

From: D. E. Butler and J. Freeman *British Political Facts, 1900–1966,* 1967

EXTRACT E   *An Act to declare and amend the law relating to trade disputes and trade unions,* 29 July 1927

1.—(1) It is hereby declared—
    (a) that any strike is illegal if it—
      (i) has any object other than or in addition to the furtherance of a trade dispute within 10 the trade or industry in which the strikers are engaged; and
(ii) is a strike designed or calculated to coerce the Government either directly or indirectly or by inflicting hardship upon the community; . . .

3.—(1) It is hereby declared that it is unlawful for one
or more persons ... to attend at or near a house or
place where a person resides or works or carries on
business or happens to be, for the purpose of
15   obtaining or communicating information or of
persuading or inducing any person to work or to
abstain from working, if they attend in such
numbers or otherwise in such manner as to be
calculated to intimidate any person in that house or
20   place, or to obstruct the approach thereto or egress
therefrom, or to lead to a breach of the peace, ...
4.—(1) It shall not be lawful to require any member of
a trade union to make any contribution to the
political fund of a trade union ... unless ... he ...
25   [has given] notice in writing ... of his willingness to
contribute ...
(2) All contributions to the political fund of a trade
union from members ... shall be levied and made
separately from any contributions to the other
30   funds of the trade union and no assets of the trade
union, other than the amount raised by such a
separate levy ... shall be carried to that fund ...

17 and 18 George V, C. 22.

Questions

a   Study Extracts B and C:

(i) What differences are there in the portrayals of the
opponents of the General Strike in each of the
cartoons?   *(3)*

(ii) How does Extract B differ from Extract C in the
portrayal of the strikers and their movement? *(3)*

b   How far does Extract A accord with the views expressed in the two cartoons?   *(6)*

c   Using all the extracts: What evidence is there to
suggest that the scale of industrial action was on an
unprecedented level?   *(4)*

d   What activities of the strikers in the dispute are suggested by Extract E?   *(4)*

_____

(20 marks)

Political crisis, 1931

James Ramsay MacDonald occupied the post of Prime
Minister on three occasions, but, in each government he
formed, his own party was in a minority. The Labour
government was a minority in 1924, in 1929, when it held
only 288 seats, and in 1931, when Ramsay MacDonald held
office with his political opponents.

This limit on the Labour Party's political power occurred
in an era of social and economic unrest. As the effects of the
Wall Street Crash and general world slump worked through
the global economy so unemployment rose and balancing
the national accounts became more difficult. The immediate
solution seemed to be funding public works, but this
required loans and the creation of a budget deficit. Worries
about where such a solution might lead had seen the
creation of the May Committee which reported in July
1931. The results were hardly unanimous, but a majority of
members foresaw a deficit of £120 millions and suggested
covering this by increasing income tax and making cuts in
public spending. They suggested cutting unemployment
benefit, obviously a politically sensitive matter.

By August 1931, a separate government committee had
decided on £78 millions-worth of cuts but could only gain

agreement in Cabinet for £56 millions. It was this impasse
which created the need for quick government action. While
these debates continued, gold was flowing out of the
country because both national and international financiers
feared a British collapse along the lines of the recent ones in
Austria and Germany. MacDonald felt a solution could still
be reached if he had an overwhelming vote from his
colleagues, but when he put it to the test he gained a simple
majority in the Cabinet for his plans. Feeling that this was
not sufficient, MacDonald decided to resign but he was
persuaded not to by the King, Baldwin, and Samuel. Firm in
his belief that his policies were correct but realising they
were also alien to the majority of his party, MacDonald
bowed to persuasion and agreed to lead a National
Government. Of the 550 members of that Government
only a dozen were Labour Party supporters.

There is a key question in connection with the crisis in
1931: did MacDonald have good reason to betray his party
or was he merely mistaken and hoping to retain the position
of Prime Minister? Those loyal to the party saw him as a
traitor but MacDonald certainly believed that although his
policies were diametrically opposed to those of his party

they were the only ones that could save the nation. In the end, the controversy arose over an inability to bridge the gap between £78 millions-worth of cuts needed and the £56 millions-worth offered by the cabinet. Interestingly enough, it is by no means certain that the solution offered by MacDonald to this problem, taking personal leadership of a National Government, was as overwhelmingly import- ant as he believed it to be in 1931. The document exercise that follows deals with the issues surrounding the decisions of 1931 and the political and constitutional points that it raised.

Select Bibliography

Section A

J. P. MacKintosh, *British Prime Ministers in the Twentieth Century*, Volume I, Weidenfeld and Nicolson (1977)

A. J. P. Taylor, *English History, 1914–1945*, Oxford Univer- sity Press (1965)

Section B

R. Bassett, *1931: Political Crisis*, Macmillan (1958)

D. Marquand, *Ramsay MacDonald*, Cape (1977)

K. Rose, *King George V*, Weidenfeld and Nicolson (1983)

Essays

a Why was there a political crisis in 1931 and what were its consequences? (ODLE 85)

b Discuss the circumstances which led to the formation of the National Government in 1931. (JMB 80)

c 'The formation of a National Government in 1931 was the only possible way of signifying the gravity of the nation's economic plight.' How far do you agree? (UL 84)

Exercise Six: Unseen

Multiple extract style.   25 marks.   Time allowed: 45 minutes

EXTRACT A   Viscount Snowden, *An Autobiography*, 1934

From Thursday, 20th August to Sunday, 23rd August, Mr. MacDonald and I had frequent interviews with the Opposition. They maintained that if the government could not (make more) economies, they would unite and defeat the government. They were dissatisfied with the proposals for reducing the cost of unemployment payments....

The split in the Labour Cabinet took place on the proposal to reduce the unemployment pay by 10%. The

May Committee had recommended a cut of 20%. After a 10% cut in the unemployment pay, the recipients of these payments would still be in a better position than they were in 1924. There had been a fall in the cost of living which was equivalent to a 30% increase in the purchasing power of the benefits.

'The Cabinet would not agree to implement the authority they had given us to submit suggestions to the Opposition leaders, and the bankers. A small majority were in favour of these economies, but, as half the Cabinet would have resigned, the break-up of the Labour Government was inevitable....'

EXTRACT B   Hugh Dalton, *Call Back Yesterday: Memoirs 1886–1931*, 1953

... MacDonald sits alone on the other side of the long table ... he has to tell us that the Government is at an end. He is very sorry. We shall curse him, and he is afraid that he has caused us great embarrassment. But the gravity of the crisis is not yet widely understood....

He thinks the crisis could have been avoided if the Cabinet hadn't changed its mind at a critical point. A plan had been drawn up and agreed, which would have sufficed to secure the loan required. But then the Cabinet went back on it. ... this made necessary a Government of Persons, not Parties. He is going through with this. ... all members of the government will resign together, and then the new administration will be formed....

And then we disperse. Going out, Willy Lunn and I speak vigorously against J.R.M. And I apparently am clearly audible. ... There are lot of pressmen outside. ... To one pressman I say 'Just for a handful of panic he left us.'

EXTRACT C   H. Boardman, *The Glory of Parliament*, 1960

On Sunday night, August 23, the drama came to its climax. The Cabinet prepared for all other economies, split on a ten per cent cut in unemployment benefit. It was long believed that there was a majority against the cut, but it has been established that there was a majority of either one or two for it. MacDonald decided that the minority was too great to permit him to carry on. He left his Cabinet colleagues to go to Buckingham Palace with the intention, as they understood it, of resigning. One of his colleagues described him as being jaunty. The King's Secretary, Sir Clive Wigram, speaks of him arriving at Buckingham Palace 'scared and unbalanced'. ... MacDonald returned from the Palace to tell his colleagues that he had undertaken, supported by Baldwin and Samuel, to lead a National Government....

The Twentieth Century

EXTRACT D Harold Laski, *Parliamentary Government,* 1938

It is notable that, in the formation of the National Government, no attempt was made by the King to elicit the views of the great bulk of the Labour Party who transferred their allegiance from Mr. MacDonald to Mr. Arthur Henderson. It appears certain that the impetus to the peculiar form of the new administration came wholly from the King. Mr. MacDonald was as much the personal choice of George V as Lord Bute was the personal choice of George III. He is the sole modern Prime Minister who has been unencumbered by party support in his period of office; he provided only a name, while Mr. Baldwin supplied both the legions and the power that goes with the legions. We need not doubt that the King acted as he did wholly from a conception of patriotic obligation. But since it is known that a Baldwin Premiership was confidently expected at least as late as the night before the break-up of the Labour Government, it is not, I think, unreasonable to term Mr. Ramsay MacDonald's emergence as Prime Minister of the National Government a Palace Revolution.

EXTRACT E Kenneth Rose, *King George V,* 1983

It is true that on three separate occasions—on Sunday morning, on Sunday night and on Monday morning—the King persuaded his Prime Minister not to resign. But persuasion is not unconstitutional; indeed, it is a royal prerogative. Had MacDonald persisted in his wish to resign, the King could not have prevented him. It was on the advice of the Prime Minister, moreover, that the King consulted Samuel and Baldwin on the Sunday morning and summoned them to a conference with MacDonald at the palace twenty-four hours later; it was on the advice of the Prime Minister that the King then accepted their joint plan for a National Government. ... Speed was essential. Almost hour by hour, the country's gold and currency reserves were draining away as foreign investors lost confidence. The King was thus denied the conventional course of action: to accept the Prime Minister's resignation and so set in motion the machinery for a general election. There was no time to seek the opinion of the electorate through the ballot box. Within constitutional limits, the King had to use his own discretion in finding an emergency Government stable enough both to encourage Britain's creditors and to command a parliamentary majority that could pass the necessary measures of retrenchment.

The choice was limited. One course was to accept MacDonald's resignation and send for the next senior member of his party. But Henderson, the leader of those Labour ministers opposed to drastic economies, would neither inspire confidence abroad nor retain a parliamentary majority over the combined Conservative and Liberal Parties. A more practical alternative was for the King to accept MacDonald's resignation and send for Baldwin, as leader of the next largest party in the Commons. With Liberal support, Baldwin could certainly have formed an administration strong enough to carry out a programme of retrenchment. But the King decided to go one better. He induced MacDonald to lead the new ministry and so proclaim to the world that Britain spoke with a united and resolute voice in her determination to remain solvent.

Questions

a Using Extracts A and B:

(i) What agreement is there over the role of the Cabinet in forcing the crisis? *(3)*

(ii) What indications are there that economic factors played a major part in the actions of politicians in 1931? *(3)*

(iii) What political pressures were being exerted on the Labour leaders? *(3)*

b What evidence is there in Extract C to support Laski's contention in Extract D about the role of the King in the formation of the National Government? *(3)*

c Using Extract E:

(i) How far is Boardman's contention in Extract C, that MacDonald was intending to resign, supported by evidence in Extract E? *(3)*

(ii) How does Rose refute Laski's arguments put forward in Extract D that the idea for the new administration 'come wholly from the King'? *(3)*

(iii) Explain why the King agreed to the formation of a National Government. *(7)*

(25 marks)

52

Appeasement and the coming of war

Germany's defeat in 1918 and the Treaty of Versailles were the final blows in the beating Germany had received since the start of war in 1914. Germany had fallen from being an example of Imperial splendour and the subject of world envy to abject defeat and ruin in the space of four years. Attempts to wring the last drops of blood from the Wilhelmine corpse at Versailles were not supported by all delegates, some of whom realised the necessity of being magnanimous in victory. Although these men succeeded in tempering some of the impositions of the Treaty most clauses were agreed upon with a plain disregard for the future recovery and well-being of Germany.

After 1919 it was certainly realised by most statesmen that Germany would have to be rehabilitated, at least diplomatically, if not economically. The process was slow and fraught with obvious prejudices towards the country that had, supposedly, thrown Europe into turmoil and war. However, with American aid, the Locarno Treaties, and Germany's entry into the League of Nations it seemed as though her rehabilitation was complete. It was only with the fall of the Weimar Republic and the rise of Adolf Hitler that the European nations had to decide on how to deal with an aggressive German foreign policy. Certainly, no one wanted European war, the carnage of 1914–18 was too fresh in people's minds, but neither could blatant contraventions of international law be tolerated. The concept of appeasement, giving way to justified demands, invited Hitler to try his luck time and again. Rearmament, re-occupation of the Rhineland, the Anschluss, and Czechoslovakia all occurred because of appeasement. If events had been halted at Czechoslovakia then possibly historians would be more charitable to the policy and the man identified with it, Neville Chamberlain. However, Czech- 5 oslovakia was followed by Poland and as soon as Poland went to war with Germany the complete failure of appeasement was demonstrated. Why Britain did not use force before 1939 is a complex question. In part, it is answered by Chamberlain's commitment to appeasement and his ab- 10 horrence of war, but it is also true to say that Britain felt itself unprepared for conflict in the years preceding 1939. It is this last point which is raised in the document question that follows that deals with the reasons for Britain's reluctance to force international issues in the years leading 15 up to the outbreak of the Second World War.

Select Bibliography

Section A

R. Henig, *Origins of the Second World War*, Methuen (1985)
W. R. Rock, *Appeasement in the 1930s*, Edward Arnold (1977)

Section B

A. P. Adamthwaite, *The Making of the Second World War*, Allen & Unwin (1979)
H. Montgomery Hyde, *Neville Chamberlain*, Weidenfeld and Nicolson (1976)
A. J. P. Taylor, *Origins of the Second World War*, Hamish Hamilton (1961)
K. G. Robbins, *Munich*, Cassell (1968)
C. Thorne, *The Approach of War, 1938–39*, Macmillan (1967)

Essays

a What was the case for Appeasement in the 1930s? (OCSEB 82)
b Who won and who lost at the Munich Conference of 1938? (UCLES Sp. Sub. 83)
c Compose a speech by a Conservative MP in the censure debate of 7–8 May either defending or attacking the conduct of Chamberlain as Prime Minister. (ODLE 84)

Exercise Seven: Seen

Multiple extract style.   25 marks.   Time allowed: 45 minutes

EXTRACT A   *Neville Chamberlain's Diary*, 20 March 1938

... with Franco winning in Spain with the aid of German guns and Italian planes, with a French Government in which one cannot have the slightest confidence and which I suspect to be close-ish touch with our Opposition, with the Russians stealthily and cunningly pulling all the strings behind the scenes to get us involved in war with Germany ... and finally with Germany flushed with triumph, and all too conscious of her power, the prospect looked black indeed. ... You only have to look at the map to see that nothing that France or we could do could possibly save Czechoslovakia from being overrun by the Germans, if they wanted to do it. The Austrian frontier is practically open; the great Skoda munitions works are within easy bombing distance of the German aerodromes, the railways all pass through German territory, Russia is 100 miles away. Therefore we could not help Czechoslovakia—she would simply be a pretext for going to war with Germany. That we could not think of unless we had a reasonable prospect of beating her to her knees in a reasonable time, and of that I see no sign. ...

EXTRACT B   A. J. P. Taylor, *Origins of the Second World War*, 1961

Moreover, on 19 September, Benes asked two questions of the Soviet Union: 'Will the U.S.S.R. render immediate effective assistance if France remains true and also renders assistance? Will the U.S.S.R. assist Czech-
5 oslovakia, as a member of the League of Nations, in accordance with Articles 16 and 17?' On 20 September the Soviet government replied to the first question: 'Yes, instantly and effectively'; to the second: 'Yes, in every respect.'

EXTRACT C

Table 1 Land forces (strengths, expressed in divisions, are war strengths)

	January 1938	August 1939
Germany	81[1]	120–30
Italy	73	73
France	63	86
Great Britain	2	4[2]
USSR	125	125
Czechoslovakia	34	—
Poland	40	40

Notes: [1] This figure included twenty-four *Landwehr* divisions which were not fully trained or equipped.

    [2] Maximum force immediately available for service overseas.

Table 2 Air strengths (in numbers of aircraft of all types—for Great Britain, France and Italy metropolitan strengths only are given)

	January 1938	August 1939
Germany	1,820	4,210
Italy	1,301	1,531
France	1,194	1,234
Great Britain	1,053	1,750
USSR	3,050	3,361
Czechoslovakia	600	—
Poland	500	500

From: A. P. Adamthwaite, *The Making of the Second World War*, 1979

EXTRACT D   Winston Churchill, *The Second World War*, 1949

The subjugation of Czechoslovakia robbed the Allies of the Czech Army of twenty-one regular divisions, fifteen or sixteen second-line divisions already mobilised, and

also their mountain fortress line which, in the days of
5 Munich, had required the deployment of thirty German divisions, or the main strength of the mobile and fully-trained German Army. According to Generals Halder and Jodl there were but thirteen German divisions, of which only five were composed of first-line troops, left
10 in the West at the time of the Munich arrangement. We certainly suffered a loss through the fall of Czech-oslovakia equivalent to some thirty-five divisions. Besides this the Skoda works, the second most important arsenal in central Europe, the production of which
15 between August, 1938, and September, 1939, was in itself nearly equal to the actual output of British arms factories in that period, was made to change sides adversely. While all Germany was working under intense and almost war pressure, French Labour had
20 achieved as early as 1936 the long desired forty-hours week.

EXTRACT E   Terms of the Russo-German Agreement, August 1939

… Both High contracting parties obligate themselves to desist from any act of violence, any aggressive action, and any attack on each other, either individually or jointly with other powers.

EXTRACT F   Winston Churchill, ibid

The Germans had in fact done most of their air expansion both in quantity and quality before the war began. Our effort was later than theirs by nearly two years. Between 1939 and 1940 they made a twenty per
5 cent increase only, whereas our increase in modern fighter aircraft was eighty per cent. The year 1938 in fact found us sadly deficient in quality, and although by 1939 we had gone some way towards meeting the disparity we were still relatively worse off than in 1940,
10 when the test came.

    We might in 1938 have had air raids on London, for which we were lamentably unprepared. There was however no possibility of a decisive Air Battle of Britain until the Germans had occupied France and the
15 Low Countries, and thus obtained the necessary bases in close striking distance of our shores. Without these bases they could not have escorted their bombers with the fighter aircraft of those days. The German armies were not capable of defeating the French in 1938 or
20 1939.

Questions

a Using Extract A explain the reasons Chamberlain had for not fighting a war against Germany over Czechoslovakia in 1938. *(6)*

b What evidence is there in Extract B that throws doubts on Chamberlain's assessments in Extract A? *(3)*

c Using Extracts C and D explain how Britain's military position *vis à vis* Germany had worsened by the end of 1939. *(8)*

d Using Extracts E and F explain:

(i) How Britain may have suffered in a conflict started in 1939. *(4)*

(ii) How Churchill thought Chamberlain's caution in Extract A was unwarranted. *(4)*

(25 marks)

The Battle of Britain, 1940

'Never in the field of human conflict was so much owed by so many to so few.' This was how Winston Churchill summed up the role of the Royal Air Force in successfully defending Britain from a German aerial assault in the late summer and autumn of 1940. Hitler's hopes of reaching an agreement with Britain after the Fall of France were short lived. This created a problem for him. If he attempted to take on Britain he might well find himself in a protracted conflict, stretching from the British Isles to Egypt, putting his own resources under considerable strain. However, left alone, Britain could well become an important base for a new war between America and Germany.

Hitler decided to attack but the German navy, badly weakened by operations in Norway, simply did not have the number of ships necessary to cover an invasion. The solution seemed simple; utilise the highly-trained and successful Luftwaffe to knock out British fighter defences and prepare the way for a combined army and naval invasion. On the eve of the Battle of Britain, in early July, Germany had a slight numerical advantage over Britain in single-engined fighters. However, Britain's Spitfires were marginally superior, she was building planes at a quicker rate, and pilots forced to bale out would do so over their own territory and could come into service again immediately. Britain also had a Radio Direction Finding defence system which supplemented the sterling work of the Observer Corps. After aerial battles in the first week of the conflict, the German forces turned their attention to a far more damaging tactic of bombing radar stations and fighter and bomber squadrons. This was hampered by bad weather for some days and the difficulty of successfully destroying the tall radar masts. In addition the Luftwaffe failed to recognise the significance of the radar defence systems and throughout the conflict a blanket cover was maintained. The change of tack by the Luftwaffe to bombing cities rather than Bomber Command was based on the false belief that Britain's Air Force was on its last legs and because Bomber Command had already started to attack German cities. Although some devastating raids followed, Hitler never gave the command to invade and after the events of 15 September he decided to call off his plans. On that day the German Air Force was severely beaten, losing far more planes than the RAF, and it failed on two further occasions to win the supremacy of the skies above Britain. Although air attacks continued, the attempt to secure German air supremacy with a view to invasion had been beaten off. The document exercise follows the events of the Battle of Britain and the eventual victory for the RAF against the German Luftwaffe.

Select Bibliography

Section A

B. H. Lidell Hart, *History of the Second World War*, Cassell (1970)

Section B

B. Collier, *The Battle of Britain*, Jackdaw No. 65 (1969)

L. Deighton, *Fighter: The True Story of the Battle of Britain*, Panther (1978)

R. J. Overy, *Goering: The Iron Man*, Routledge (1984)

J. Terraine, *The Right of the Line: The RAF in European War, 1939–1945*, Hodder & Stoughton (1985)

Essays

a What contribution was made by the British and American Air Forces to victory in Europe in the Second World War? (JMB 84)

b 'The Bomber will always get through'. What effect did this view have on British strategy in Europe during the period 1936–45? (AEB)

c Discuss the successes and failures of British air power in the Second World War. (UCLES 84)

Exercise Eight: Seen

Multiple extract style.   20 marks.   Time allowed: 40 minutes

EXTRACT A   *Punch*, 7 February 1940

COMING SHORTLY
OR
ADOLF THE AWFUL IN HIS AMAZING AERIAL ACT

EXTRACT B   *Punch*, 12 June 1940

LITTLE ADOLF HEAD-IN-AIR

EXTRACT C   Winston Churchill, *The Second World War*, Vol. II, 1949

The Air Marshal himself walked up and down behind, watching with vigilant eye every move in the game, supervising his junior executive hand, and only occasionally intervening with some decisive order,
5 usually to reinforce a threatened area. In a little while all our squadrons were fighting, and some had already begun to return for fuel. All were in the air. The lower line of bulbs was out (one for each fighter station). There was not one squadron left in reserve. . . . The
10 odds were great; our margins small; the stakes infinite.

EXTRACT D   Peter Calvocoressi and Guy Wint, *Total War: Causes and Courses of the Second World War*, 1972

In July 1940 Generals Kesselring and Sperrle, commanding Luftflotten 2 and 3 in Belgium and Northern France, and General Stumpf, commanding Luftflotten 5 in Denmark and Norway, had a front line strength of
5 around 3,000 aircraft, including some 1,400 long-range bombers, 300 dive-bombers, 800 single-engined fighters and 280 twin-engined fighters or fighter bombers. Of this force, 2,500 aircraft at the most were serviceable and ready for action at the beginning of the battle. . . .
10   . . . The RAF's front line strength on the eve of the Battle of Britain was 1,200. It included 800 Hurricane and Spitfire single seater fighters, of which 660 were operational, and in this sphere the British were roughly equal in numbers to the units opposed to them.
15 Reserves were healthy and production good. . . .

Questions

a   Where had the German airforce proved itself in the years before 1939?   *(2)*

b   Taking into account the dates, comment on the portrayals of Hitler in Extracts A and B.   *(4)*

c   What is the significance of the British ships in Extract B and how had the Royal Navy affected Hitler's plans for Operation Sea-Lion?   *(4)*

d   What evidence is there in Extract C to suggest that Extract B was an optimistic portrayal of events in 1940?   *(2)*

e   How far does Extract D bear out Churchill's description in Extract C?   *(2)*

f   Why did Germany fail to defeat Britain in the air in 1940?   *(6)*

(20 marks)

Suez, 1956

Colonel Nasser took over as Egyptian leader from General Neguib in 1954. He was determined to make Egypt the spearhead in the Arab front against Israel and to 'play-off' the East and West against each other. This dangerous game went badly awry in 1956. Nasser had solicited both US and Russian loans for the building of the High Dam at Aswan. However, when he tried to secure the American loan, his proposal was met with a rejection from both America and Britain. Nasser was incensed and nationalised the Suez Canal on 26 July 1956, declaring that the profits would be used to finance the High Dam. By taking control, Nasser had dispossessed the French company that owned and operated the Canal.

Both Britain and France were offended by Nasser's high-handed action, which in their view, was no less than international theft. Both nations made plans for military intervention. The British Prime Minister, Eden, felt his actions were justified, as Nasser's act was a threat to the livelihood of nations and would have prevented free passage through the Canal. The Anglo-French action was intent upon at least freeing the Canal Zone from Nasser's grip and there was the implied threat of toppling Nasser from power as well, although initial plans to strike at Alexandria and Cairo were modified to a mere seizure of the Canal Zone. While the British and French were preparing military actions, the Americans were taking a more detached view. They favoured a peaceful solution, although were also concerned to return the Canal to international hands rather than have its future dictated by Nasser. The issue was complicated by an Israeli announcement to the French that they intended to attack Egypt or Jordan soon in retaliation for terrorist attacks. After a secret meeting in Paris, the attack went ahead on 29 October 1956 and on the following day the British and the French demanded a withdrawal of Egyptian forces from the Canal. The Egyptian refusal invited attack which was halted after four days by the weight of international criticism moving against France and Britain at the United Nations. A series of resolutions saw the despatch of a peace-keeping force and an end to hostilities.

By this time, the Canal had been blocked and the subsequent rise in oil prices cost Britain dearly, allowing America to pressure her into submission. The political ramifications in Britain were severe, with resignations from the Cabinet and Eden's eventual departure. However, the greatest sufferer was British prestige which fell remarkably, especially in the eyes of the Middle Eastern countries. The document exercise that follows outlines some of the events surrounding the Suez Crisis in 1956.

Select Bibliography

Section A

A. Sked and C. Cook, *Post-War Britain: A Political History,* Penguin (1979)

Section B

S. Aster, *Anthony Eden,* Weidenfeld and Nicolson (1976)

D. Hopwood, *Egypt: Politics and Society 1945–1984,* Allen & Unwin (1982)

H. Thomas, *The Suez Affair,* Weidenfeld and Nicolson (1967)

K. M. Wilson (ed.), *Imperialism and Nationalism in the Middle East: The Anglo-Egyptian Experience 1882–1982,* Mansell (1983)

Essays

a How far did the Suez Crisis of 1956 compel a reassessment of Britain's role in world affairs? (UCLES 82)

b What were the origins of the Suez Crisis and what were its consequences for Britain? (OCSEB 82)

c 'The Suez Crisis of 1956 marked the end of Great Britain as an independent world power.' Discuss. (ODLE 82)

Exercise Nine: Unseen

Multiple extract style.   20 marks.   Time allowed: 40 minutes

EXTRACT A   Letter from President Eisenhower to Eden, September 1956, *Eisenhower Memoirs*

Dear Anthony,

... We have a grave problem confronting us in Nasser's reckless adventure with the canal, and I do not differ from you in your estimate of his intentions and purposes. The place where we apparently do not agree
5   is on the probable effects in the Arab world of the various possible reactions by the Western World. You seem to believe that any long, drawn out controversy ... will inevitably make Nasser an Arab hero. ... This, I think, is a picture too dark ... I believe ... we can
10 expect the Arabs to rally firmly to Nasser's support [if] ... there should be a resort to force without thoroughly exploring and exhausting every possible peaceful means of settling the issue. ... Nasser thrives on drama. If we let some of the drama go out of the situation and
15 concentrate upon ... deflating him through slower but sure processes (such as economic pressures, Arab rivalries, a new pipe-line to Turkey, more oil for Europe from Venezuela) ... I assure you we are not blind to the fact that eventually there may be no escape from the
20 use of force. ... But to resort to military action when

the world believes there are other means available ...
would set in motion forces that could lead ... to the
most distressing results....

EXTRACT B   Hugh Thomas, *The Suez Affair*, 1970

One fact dominated US reaction to Suez; it was election
year. Eisenhower, who at sixty-six had recovered from
his bad heart attack in 1955 and an intestinal operation
that June, was standing for re-election in November,
5   and as the Prince of Peace. Only 15 per cent of US oil
imports came through the Suez Canal. While the route
to Europe from the Persian Gulf via the Cape was two
thirds longer than via the Canal, to the USA it was only
two-fifths. US investments in the Canal Company itself
10   were negligible....

EXTRACT C   Sir Anthony Eden, Statement in the
House of Commons, 30 October 1956

... news was received last night that Israeli forces had
crossed the frontier and had penetrated deep into
Egyptian territory.... Her Majesty's government and
the French government have accordingly agreed that
5   everything possible should be done to bring hostilities
to an end as soon as possible ... in seeking an immediate meeting of the Security Council.... In the mean-
time, as a result of the consultations held in London
today, the United Kingdom and French Governments
10   have now addressed an urgent communication to the
Governments of Egypt and Israel. In these we have
called upon both sides to stop all warlike actions by

land, sea and air forthwith and to withdraw their
military forces to a distance of 10 miles from the canal.
15   Further, in order to separate the belligerents and to
guarantee freedom of transit through the canal by the
ships of all nations, we have asked the Egyptian
government to agree that Anglo-French forces should
move temporarily – I repeat, temporarily – into key
20   positions at Port Said, Ismailia, and Suez.

The governments of Egypt and Israel have been
asked to answer this communication within twelve
hours. It has been made clear to them that, if at the
expiration of that time one or both have not undertaken
25   to comply with these requirements, British and French
forces will intervene in whatever strength may be
necessary to secure compliance.

EXTRACT D   *Sydney Morning Herald* (date unknown)

From: E. Raynor *et al*, *Evidence in Question: International
Affairs since 1919*, OUP (1980)

EXTRACT E   The Earl of Avon, *The Eden Memoirs:
Full Circle*, 1960

The General Assembly of the United Nations met on
the morning of November 2nd. Sir Pierson Dixon
rehearsed the case for our police action with his
customary clarity and vigour. But the Assembly was in
5   an emotional mood. There was talk of collective action
against the French and ourselves. ... It was not Soviet
Russia, or any Arab state, but the Government of the
United States which took the lead in the Assembly
against Israel, France and Britain. The Secretary of State
10   said he moved the resolution with a heavy heart. It
took no account whatever of events preceding the
action. ... There was no suggestion of going to the
root of the matter, or of using the Anglo-French
intervention to good purpose, either to create an
15   effective international force, or to negotiate ... an
international agreement for the canal....

The resolution put peace in a strait-jacket. Directed
against Anglo-French intervention as well as fighting, it
declared that all parties ... should agree to an
20   immediate cease-fire....

Questions

a   What were the two main lines of policy foreseen by
President Eisenhower in Extract A, and how did he see
their eventual outcome?   *(6)*

b   Using Extracts B and C:

(i)   Why might America have viewed the closing of the
Suez Canal with less alarm than Britain or France?
(3)

(ii)   What reasons did Eden give for introducing
Anglo-French forces into key areas?   *(3)*

c   How might Eden have been reasonably expected to
have foreseen the outcome of the military action as
described in Extract E?   *(6)*

d   How far is the cartoon extract a reasonable commen-
tary on the outcome of Eden's policy and decision?

(2)

(20 marks)

Specimen answers: Anglo-German naval rivalry

a The OberKommando states that maritime nations need to protect their maritime interests, such as colonial possessions, trade routes for both imports of raw materials and exports of finished goods, and fishing grounds. It is also suggested in Extract A that nations may deem it necessary to protect their maritime interests whenever they are threatened, such as in international conflicts, and for this purpose a strong navy is of paramount importance.

b (i) In Extract B, the relative sizes of Queen Victoria and little 'Willie' reflect not only their family relationship but also the established power of England and the growing might of Germany. There is some suggestion of England crowing over its possession of a navy and a hint of the beginning of a jealous reaction by Germany at not having a fleet.

In Extract C, the cartoonist seems to be making a more open comment showing Edward's large navy being challenged by the growing, although smaller, German navy. Edward's comment suggests that he is belittling the size of the navy by suggesting that the Kaiser treat it as something of a diversion rather than major project.

(ii) The English cartoon, Extract D, suggests that Germany now enjoys at least an equal standing with Britain as far as naval strength goes, with a dejected John Bull looking on at Germany flaunting her new naval power. However, the figures in Extract E suggest a different story. Although Germany's navy is increasing in size this growth is steady rather than exponential and does not match Britain's building programme in battleships and Dreadnoughts. In fact, throughout the period 1907 to 1911 Britain maintained a fairly constant lead of about *double* the number of German battleships and Dreadnoughts. So, although Germany was now an important naval power she certainly had not usurped Britain's control of the seas.

c In Extract F, Von Stumm suggests that German naval power is not necessarily designed to be strong enough to defeat Britain but certainly will make Britain wary of Germany and perhaps persuade her to talk rather than to fight. However, Extract E indicates that there was a continual race in naval building from 1907 to 1911. Britain seems to be coping with the 'heavy financial burdens' of Dreadnought building, mentioned by Von Stumm. Extract G also casts doubts on the idea of an English-initiated naval agreement with Germany on the basis of England's fear of German competition in this sphere. Sir Edward Grey states that a navy is essential to Britain's very existence, whereas for Germany a strong navy was something of a luxury. So both Extracts E and G would suggest that Von Stumm had incorrectly calculated the likely impact of a growth in German naval power *vis à vis* Britain. Instead of drawing her to the negotiating table it had forced her back to the shipyards.

However, Von Stumm was not wrong in all of his predictions. He suggests that Britain harboured a desire to maintain a 100 per cent advantage in numbers of ships over Germany, something which he believed Britain could not do. Certainly, in Extract G, Grey merely states that Britain would not tolerate a German navy that was 'superior to ours' without mentioning anything about specific ratios. Extract E also suggests that by 1911, at least as far as battleships were concerned, Britain could not maintain a 100 per cent advantage over Germany.

Therefore, the points that Von Stumm outlines seem to have some validity for the naval 'numbers game' in the years up to 1911 but his belief that Britain would negotiate rather than take up the challenge thrown down by Germany is not substantiated by the evidence in Extracts E and G.

Specimen answers: Ireland, 1912–14

a In Extract A Carson states that Home Rule will be disastrous for Ireland and, in particular, for the material well-being of Ulster. He also indicates that Home Rule will establish a precedent that could endanger the unity of the Empire.

b Kipling gives a Protestant view of the Catholic Church which suggests that Catholics see themselves as having sole right to salvation and by implication refusing salvation to adherents of other churches. Hence Ulster's defiance is not only a statement of political independence but also religious faith.

c Kipling's poem appears to foresee a far more immediate and belligerent struggle than Carson does. Kipling refers directly to the 'war prepared' between Ulster Protestants and Irish Catholics should Home Rule be declared. Kipling emphasises the religious dimensions in the struggle and the almost inevitable violence it will bring. Carson appears to be less emotional in his pronouncements, although no less vehement in his rejection of Home Rule by referring to Ulster's ties with England and the King, a desire to preserve the unity of the Empire, and a total rejection of any proposal for an Irish Parliament. Both Carson and Kipling are equally assured of one thing, and that is, Ulster's complete opposition to the proposed plans for Home Rule. They share a determination to fight, 'using all means necessary', in Carson's words, to protect Ulster's identity.

d   In Extract C, Carson suggests that Westminster could follow one of two approaches to solve the Home Rule problem. Firstly, Westminster could try to force Ulster to submit. Secondly, Westminster could try to bring Ulster round to believe that Home Rule would result in 'good' government.

e   Extract D suggests that with the loyalty of four out of every ten soldiers in doubt, any attempt to enforce Home Rule by the use of the army would be quite foolish and would invite rejection and possible mutiny. This delicate state of affairs was made more complex by the suggestion that the Ulster Volunteer forces should be offered to England in the event of war. It would then be very difficult to have regular army detachments, if any could be found, enforcing unpopular legislation on an apparently loyal body of men.

f   (i)   When introduced in 1912, Home Rule provided for a separate Irish Parliament in Dublin to deal with specifically Irish affairs. Westminster would still take decisions on defence and foreign policy. However, as these decisions would affect their lives, the Irish would be allowed to send forty-two MPs to Westminster to represent their interests. Such a proposal was totally opposed by Ulstermen and after repeated failures to gain House of Lords support for Home Rule, and the difficulties raised by the Curragh incident, Asquith tried to secure Lord's assent for a proposal to exclude certain Ulster districts for six years if they desired it.

(ii)   Although Asquith proposed to exclude, temporarily or even permanently, four Northern Counties, this compromise was one that was totally unacceptable to both Ulster and the rest of Ireland. Hence, its suggestion and proposed implementation would have invited criticism from not only Ulster but all of Ireland and so successfully ended any chances of concerted action over Home Rule.

(iii)   The outbreak of the European crisis in the summer of 1914, following the assassination of Archduke Francis Ferdinand, made it necessary to shelve Home Rule in the face of greater potential dangers. Home Rule legislation was suspended for the duration of the war and by the end of hostilities new forces in Irish politics had arisen to block the path of Home Rule.

Russia, 1905

The attempts to curtail the activities of revolutionary groups in Russia in the latter part of the nineteenth century had only been partially successful. Political opponents both in Russia and outside survived. However, the unrest witnessed in 1905 was caused by a ground-swell of general discontent in the country, more than organised political revolution. The rapid rate of Russian industrialisation had resulted in appalling working and living conditions for many town-dwellers who suffered from low wages, long hours, and disease. They felt further resentment because of the government's control of their lives, their lack of political representation, and the waste and corruption they saw in government.

Fuelled by further discontent as a result of the disastrous events in the unsuccessful war against Japan with its humiliating defeats, loss of men, and associated mutinies, the Russian workers in St Petersburg gave full vent to their anger and exasperation. Although the police authorities tried to channel discontent into peaceful workers' organis-ations these often grew into more militant groups. One such group was led by Georgi Gapon, previously a police agent. This group decided to march through the streets to the Winter Palace in order to put their grievances before the Tsar himself. They intended to present a statement of their complaints and expected no less than justice from their paternal ruler. The Tsar was not even at the palace on Sunday 22 January when the procession approached. Uncertain of how the crowd might react, and fearing a riot, the soldiers opened fire and killed many of the protestors. Most important of all, the trust of the Russian people in the Tsar, which had helped to maintain the monarchy in the past, was shattered. Widespread unrest followed and was countered by repression but the outcry would not die down. Strikes proliferated and workers, under the leadership of men such as Trotsky, took a prominent role. A General Strike was threatened and more violence did not seem to be the answer. Witte's insistent advice was reluctantly accepted by the Tsar, who decided to grant the

October Manifesto. In the ensuing period of elections and the setting-up of the new system he hoped to be able to re-establish a firm grip on his country. The Manifesto was an offer of peace and its promise of elections was eagerly grasped by the Tsar's opponents but all the time the plan was to emasculate and manipulate future Dumas to ensure the continuance of Tsarist rule as unfettered from popular control as ever. The document exercise that follows traces the events of 1905 in Russia from fateful 'Bloody Sunday' to the issuing of the Manifesto.

Select Bibliography

Section A

D. Floyd, *Russia in Revolt: 1905—the First Crack in Tsarist Power*, Macdonald (1969)

L. Kochan, *The Making of Modern Russia*, Penguin (1963)

A. Wood, *The Russian Revolution*, Seminar Studies in History Series, Longman (1979)

Section B

R. D. Charques, *The Twilight of Imperial Russia*, Oxford University Press (1974)

E. Crankshaw, *The Shadow of the Winter Palace—the Drift to Revolution 1825–1917*, Penguin (1978)

L. Kochan, *Russia in Revolution*, Paladin (1970)

H. Rogger, *Russia in the Age of Modernisation and Revolution 1881–1917*, Longman (1983)

Essays

a 'The lessons of 1904–05 were plain: Russia had to avoid war, modify its autocracy, and secure social and economic reforms.' To what extent had Nicholas II learnt these lessons by 1914? (JMB 82)

b Compare the attempts made by Witte and Stolypin to preserve Tsarist autocracy. (ODLE 85)

c What were the strengths of Tsardom under Nicholas II? Was there any reason to suppose in 1905 that it would collapse within a dozen years? (AEB 83)

Exercise One: Unseen

Multiple extract.   20 marks.   Time allowed: 40 minutes

EXTRACT A   Part of workers' petition presented to the Tsar, 22 January, 1905

Sire: We, working men and inhabitants of St Petersburg, our wives and our children and our helpless old parents, have come to You to seek truth, justice, and protection. ... Sire: we have no more strength. Our endurance is at
5 an end. We have reached that terrible moment when death would be better than the prolongation of intolerable sufferings. ... Therefore we have stopped work and told our masters that we shall not start again until they comply with our demands. We ask but little.
10 We want only what is indispensable for life. ... Our first request was that our employers should discuss our demands with us, but this they refused to do. ... They regarded as illegal our other demands: reduction of the working day to eight hours, the fixing of the wage rates
15 in consultation with us, investigation of our grievances against the factory managements, an increase in the daily rate for unskilled working men and women to one rouble, the abolition of overtime, medical attention to be given carefully and considerately, and the construc-
20 tion of factories in which it is possible to work without risk of death from wind, rain and snow. ... We have been enslaved, with the help and co-operation of Your officials. Anyone who dares to speak up in defence of the interests of the working class and the ordinary
25 people is gaoled or exiled. ... Government by bureau-cracy has brought the country to complete ruin, involved it in a shameful war, and is leading further towards disaster. ... Popular representation is essential. ... Capitalists, workers, bureaucrats, priests, doctors, and
30 teachers—let them all choose their own representatives. Let them all have a free and equal vote, and for this purpose order the election of a constituent assembly on the basis of universal suffrage. ... But if You do not give these orders or respond to our pleas, we shall die
35 here in this square in front of your palace. We have nowhere else to go and there is no point in our going. There are only two paths ahead for us: one leading to freedom and happiness, the other to the grave. Let our lives be a sacrifice for suffering Russia. We do not offer
40 this sacrifice grudgingly but gladly.

From: D. Floyd, *Russia in Revolt*, 1969

EXTRACT B   Lenin (ed.), *Vperyod*, No. 4, 31 January 1905, Geneva

Most important historic events are taking place in Russia. The proletariat has risen against Tsarism. The proletariat has been driven to the uprising by the Government. Now, there is hardly room for doubt that
5 the Government deliberately allowed the strike movement to develop and a wide demonstration to be started in order to bring matters to a head, and to have a pretext for calling out the military forces. Its manoeuvre was successful. Thousands of killed and
10 wounded—this is the toll of Bloody Sunday, January 22, in Petersburg. ... The revolution is spreading. The government is already beginning to waver. From a policy of bloody repression it is trying to pass to economic concessions and to save itself by throwing a
15 sop, by promising the nine-hour day. But the lesson of Bloody Sunday must not be forgotten. The demand of the rebellious Petersburg workers—the immediate

convocation of a Constituent Assembly on the basis of
universal, direct, equal, and secret suffrage—must
20 become the demand of all striking workers.

EXTRACT C P. Milyukov, *Russia and its Crisis,* 1905

Russia is passing through a crisis; she is sick; and her
sickness is so grave as to demand an immediate and
radical cure. Palliatives can be of no use; rather, they but
increase the gravity of the situation. To pretend that all
5 is right in Russia, except for a few 'ill-intentioned'
persons who are making all the fuss, is no longer
ridiculous, it is criminal. Upon quite peaceful and law-
abiding citizens, who never shared in any political
struggle and never had any definite political opinions,
10 the feeling begins to dawn that the system of self-
defence practised by the government precludes general
progress and the development of private initiatives, just
as forty years ago progress was precluded by the
further existence of serfdom. . . . Increased and unified as
15 they are the forces of opposition are still not strong
enough to replace the government by a violent
overthrow. But they are strong enough to make the use
of violence continuous, and by increasing this to
preclude any further peaceful work of civilization. No
20 form of government can survive . . . which possesses no
moral force and is obliged to carry all its orders into
execution by mere material force.

EXTRACT D Tsar Nicholas II in a letter to his
mother describing discussions with Count Witte about
solutions to Russia's problems, in 1905

We very often met in the early morning to part only in
the evening when night fell. There were only two ways
open: to find an energetic soldier to crush the rebellion
by sheer force. There would be time to breathe then
5 but, as likely as not, one would have to use force again
in a few months, and that would mean rivers of blood
and in the end we should be where we started.

The other way out would be to give the people their
civil rights, freedom of speech, and Press, also to have
10 all the laws confirmed by a State Duma or parliament—
that of course would be a constitution. Witte defends
this energetically. He says that while it is not without
risk, it is the only way out at the present moment.
Almost everybody I had an opportunity of consulting is
15 of the same opinion. . . . He . . . drew up a Manifesto.
We discussed it for two days and in the end, invoking
God's help, I signed it. . . . My only consolation is that
such is the will of God and this grave decision will lead
my dear Russia out of the intolerable chaos she has
20 been in for nearly a year.

From: R. Tames, *Last of the Tsars,* 1972

Questions

a Consult Extract A. What were the protestors demanding, apart from improvements in working conditions?
(4)

b Consult Extract B. How does Lenin suggest:

(i) that the 1905 Revolution was a ploy by the
government that backfired? *(2)*

(ii) that the government realised this mistake and was
trying to recover lost ground? *(2)*

c Consult Extract C. What important change has
Milyukov discerned in the relationship between the
government and the opposition forces? *(4)*

d Consult Extracts B, C, and D.

(i) What two solutions did Witte and Nicholas discuss in 1905 to bring Russia's troubles to an end?
(2)

(ii) How far did the Tsar's assessment of the solutions
offered accord with the views of Lenin, in Extract
B, and Milyukov, in Extract C? *(6)*

(20 marks)

Specimen answers are on p. 79

The outbreak of the First World War

Since the First World War, there has been international
debate amongst historians about who was to blame for the
start of the hostilities in 1914. At first, the obvious choice
was Germany, especially in the light of her signing of the
Versailles Peace Treaty with its infamous 'War Guilt' clause,

231. The evidence seemed substantial and the admission of
guilt was a final confirmation. But slowly attitudes changed,
and historians began to analyse the possibilities that other
nations were also guilty. Germany may have been forced
into an untenable position by her rivalry with Great Britain

and France's continual desire for revenge, dating from the humiliation of defeat in 1871 and the loss of Alsace and Lorraine at the Treaty of Frankfurt. Perhaps it was Austria's remorseless drive into the Balkans, thinking herself safe from reprisal because of her German friendship, that invited a national response from the Balkan States and a protective Slavonic interest from Russia. As the reality of international events took the limelight in the 1930s and 1940s so this debate mellowed into a more liberal consensus of collective guilt centred on the arms race and other reasons.

Fritz Fischer's book *Germany's Aims in the First World War* re-opened the debate with a vengeance when it was published in 1961. His opinion was that blame once again should fall fairly and squarely on Germany. He saw the outbreak of war in 1914 as inevitable and calculated, being based on Germany's desire to establish herself finally as a world power, and her aim to dominate Europe, establishing a 'Mittleeuropa', and over-shadowing Britain. For Fischer these aims were known and consciously pursued before and during the war, and the individual who carries more blame than most is the German Chancellor, Bethmann-Hollweg. Obviously, such a forceful statement invited reply. Gerhard Ritter, another German historian, refuted Fischer's ideas and particularly his interpretation of Bethmann-Hollweg's role. Since the 1960s the debate has continued with a new generation of historians having to take its stance on this complex question. There is some suggestion that historians are beginning to return to wider issues, for example L. C. F. Turner's recent interpretations in his works on the origins of the war, but Fischer's ideas and the storm that they created have certainly altered the way in which historians think about the question of blame for the start of hostilities in 1914. For the purposes of the document exercise that follows a wider outlook has been adopted, concentrating on the range of forces that played a part in the outbreak of the First World War.

Select Bibliography

Section A
F. R. Bridge, *1914: The Coming of the First World War*, Historical Association (1983)
R. Langhorne, *The Collapse of the Concert of Europe, International Politics 1890–1914*, Macmillan (1981)
L. Trainor, *The Origins of the First World War*, Heinemann (1973)
L. C. F. Turner, *Origins of the First World War*, Edward Arnold (1970)

Section B
V. R. Berghahn, *Germany and the Approach to War in 1914*, Macmillan (1973)
J. Joll, *Origins of the First World War*, Longman (1984)
H. W. Koch (ed.), *The Origins of the First World War*, Macmillan (1984)
D. C. B. Lieven, *Russia and the Origins of the First World War*, Macmillan (1983)
Z. Steiner, *Britain and the Origins of the First World War*, Macmillan (1977)

Essays

a 'A Balkan war that got out of control.' Is this an adequate appraisal of the events of 1914? (OCSEB 84)
b 'Widespread war in 1914 was the unsurprising result of the national policies of almost every country taking part in it.' How far do you agree? (UL 84)
c 'Military rather than political factors were to blame for the outbreak of the First World War.' Discuss this statement. (JMB 85)

Exercise Two: Unseen

Multiple extract style.   25 marks.   Time allowed: 45 minutes

EXTRACT A   Carlton J. H. Hayes, 'The Causes of the World War', *Encyclopaedia Britannica*, 1926

The World War was directly precipitated by certain officials of the Russian General Staff. But their conduct was a natural outcome of the criminal activity of an Austrian Foreign Minister, and this in turn was aided
5 and abetted by criminal negligence at Berlin. The egotistical William II and the addle-pated Bethmann-Hollweg gave fatal *carte blanche* to the evil Berchtold; and the decision speedily passed from diplomatists to general staffs.

Yet, we must not take too seriously a few actors who strutted on the stage of European politics in July, 1914, and who by cowardice or cunning precipitated armed conflict. They would have been quite unable to precipitate any international war, much less a World
15 War, had they not been equally with millions of common people, the more or less willing agents of immense forces which for a generation had been predisposing the world to mortal combat. The whole world was parcelled out among states whose mutual
20 distrusts and jealousies were quickened by rival nationalisms and rival imperialisms; and the existence among these states of a group of Great Powers, divided in the twentieth century into two huge armed camps, provided a mighty impetus to rival militarisms. The
25 rapid rise of nationalism in the Balkans gave a most disquieting aspect to Austro-Russian Imperial rivalry in south-eastern Europe. The stimulation of national consciousness among the subject peoples of the Austrian Empire indirectly imperilled all non-national
30 states and directly embittered the relations between Germany and Russia. The attempts of Germany to obtain a commanding position in world-trade and in

overseas dominion excited not only German nationalism but the nationalism of France and of England too,
35 and incidentally brought into lurid light the future fate
of the rich and populous basin of the historical river
Rhine. It was, indeed, characteristic of the new age that
men of business were pushing their several Governments into intense rivalry with one another, while
40 patriots were pulling and applauding and that armies
and navies were standing ready to enforce economic
interests and national honour. The world-stage was set
for a gigantic war, and the stage hands comprised not
alone a few scheming diplomats but groups of pro-
45 fessional militarists and crowds of unwitting business-
men and patriots.

EXTRACT B   Winston Churchill, *The World Crisis 1911–1918*, 1923–31

Like many others, I often summon up in my memory
the impression of those July days. The world on the
verge of its catastrophe was very brilliant. Nations and
Empires crowned with princes and potentates rose
5 majestically on every side, lapped in the accumulated
treasures of the long peace. All were fitted and
fastened—it seemed securely—into an immense
cantilever. The two mighty European systems faced
each other glittering and clanking in their panoply, but
10 with a tranquil gaze. A polite, discreet, pacific, and on
the whole sincere diplomacy spread its web of connections over both. A sentence in a despatch, an observation by an ambassador, a cryptic phrase in a Parliament
seemed sufficient to adjust from day to day the balance
15 of the prodigious structure. Words counted, and even
whispers. A nod could be made to tell. Were we after
all to achieve world security and universal peace by a
marvellous system of combinations in equipoise and of
armaments in equation, of checks and counter-checks on
20 violent action every more complex, and more delicate?
Would Europe thus marshalled, thus grouped, thus
related, unite into one universal and glorious organism
capable of receiving and enjoying in undreamed of
abundance the bounty which nature and science stood
25 hand in hand to give? The old world in its sunset was
fair to see.

EXTRACT C   Lloyd George, *War Memoirs*, 1938

When I first heard the news of the assassination of the
Grand Duke Ferdinand, I felt that it was a grave matter,
and that it might provoke serious consequences which
only the firmest and most skilful handling could prevent
5 from developing into an emergency that would involve
nations. But my fears were soon assuaged by the
complete calm with which the Rulers and diplomats of
the world seemed to regard the event. The Kaiser

departed for his usual yachting holiday in the
10 Norwegian fiords. His Chief Minister left for his usual
shooting party on his estate in Silesia. The acting Head
of the German Foreign Office went off on a honeymoon
trip. A still more reassuring fact—the military head of
the German Army, von Moltke, left for his cure in a
15 foreign spa. The President of the French Republic and
his Prime Minister were on a ceremonial visit to Russia
and only arrived back in Paris on July 29th. Our
Foreign Office preserved its ordinary tranquillity of
demeanour and thought it unnecessary to sound an
20 alarm even in the Cabinet Chamber. I remember that
some time in July, an influential Hungarian lady, whose
name I have forgotten, called upon me at 11, Downing
Street, and told me that we were taking the assassination of the Grand Duke much too quietly; that it had
25 provoked such a storm throughout the Austrian Empire
as she had never witnessed, and that unless something
were done immediately to satisfy and appease resentment, it would certainly result in war with Serbia, with
the incalculable consequences which such an operation
30 might precipitate in Europe. However, such official
reports as came to hand did not seem to justify the
alarmist view she took of the situation.

EXTRACT D   A. J. P. Taylor, *The Struggle for Mastery in Europe, 1848–1918*, 1954

Yet it would be wrong to exaggerate the rigidity of the
system of alliances or to regard the European war as
inevitable. No war is inevitable until it breaks out. The
existing alliances were all precarious. Italy was only the
5 extreme example—renewing the Triple Alliance and
making exaggerated promises of military support to
Germany on the one side; seeking to negotiate a
Mediterranean agreement with France and Great Britain
on the other. In France, the Russian alliance was
10 increasingly unpopular; it was threatened by a coalition
between Caillaux, the radical, and Jaures, the socialist,
which in the summer of 1914 seemed inevitable; both
were friendly to Germany. In England the crisis over
Home Rule was reaching its height. If it had exploded,
15 there must have followed either a radical government,
which would have been friendly to Germany, or—less
likely—a conservative government, so weak as to be
debarred from having a foreign policy. Moreover in
June 1914, the British Government at last reached
20 agreement with Germany over the Baghdad railway;
and the French had already done so in February. Both
seemed to be taking sides with Germany against Russia
in the great question of Turkey-in-Asia.

EXTRACT E   Robert Graves, describing events in early 1914 in *Goodbye to All That*, 1957

One of my last recollections at Charterhouse is a school debate on the motion 'that this house is in favour of compulsory military service'. The Empire Service League, with Earl Roberts of Kandahar, V.C., as its
5 President, sent down a propagandist in support. Only six votes out of one hundred and nineteen were noes. I was the principal opposition speaker, having recently resigned from the Officers' Training Corps in revolt against the theory of implicit obedience to orders. And
10 during a fortnight spent the previous summer at the OTC camp near Tidworth on Salisbury Plain, I had been frightened by a special display of the latest military fortifications: barbed wire entanglements, machine guns, and field artillery in action. General, now
15 Field-Marshal Sir William Robertson, who had a son at the school, visited the camp and impressed upon us that war with Germany must inevitably break out within two or three years, and that we must be prepared to take our part in it as leaders of the new forces which
20 would assuredly be called into being.

Questions

a   Consult Extract A:

   (i) What reasons does Hayes give for the outbreak of the war in 1914?   *(7)*

   (ii) Why might an historian be careful in using Hayes' thoughts on the war and its outbreak?   *(3)*

b   Extract B gives an optimistic appraisal of one of the reasons for the outbreak of the war identified by Hayes in Extract A:

   (i) What was this reason?   *(2)*

   (ii) How does Extract C help to explain Churchill's optimism?   *(5)*

c   (i) Consult Extracts B and D. How does Taylor throw doubts on Churchill's war in Extract B about European tranquility prior to 1914?   *(4)*

   (ii) Consult Extracts C and E. How do these extracts suggest that many non-politicians foresaw the coming of war in 1914?   *(4)*

   (25 marks)

The Treaty of Versailles

The signatories of the treaty that ended the conflict of 1914–18 took on a monumental task in trying to emulate the success of that other great treaty a century before, the Settlement of Vienna. The conflict of the First World War had been on a scale previously unparalleled and the Treaty of Versailles was seen as an opportunity not only to redraw the European map but also to neutralise those forces in the international community that might lead to further outbreaks of war. Neither of these was an easy task given the hatred engendered by the carnage of 1914–18. France was desperate for revenge on Germany and determined to extract as draconian a settlement as possible. There were similar feelings in Britain but the delegates at Versailles realised that Germany would have to be allowed to survive.

Under the guidance of President Wilson of America, a compromise was reached but it led to the economic ruin of Germany and gave Hitler the opportunity to use the so-called 'dictated peace' as a political rallying point in Germany in the 1920s and 1930s. The infamous 'War Guilt' clause 231 was a harsh judgement to accept. Its implied obligation to redress the balance in monetary payments, mentioned in clause 232, led to the imposition of swingeing reparations payments from 1921 until their abandonment in 1932. The Treaty of Versailles aimed to 'neutralise' Germany. Germany lost wealth and important resources, and territory with German-speaking inhabitants, and was virtually stripped of armed forces. Although allowed to keep a limited army, she was forbidden to build up an airforce, or create another navy using ships over 10,000 tons, and had other severe limitations on military materials imposed on her. Despite all this, Germany was to rise again and draw the European powers and others into global conflict once more within the space of twenty years. Advocates of even more severe limitations than those actually imposed on Germany at Versailles could, in later years, point knowingly to the resurgence of Germany under Hitler in the 1930s. Others, who had asked for more restraint at Versailles in 1919, could equally well claim that more leniency would have given Europe a workable peace that may have maintained stability and prevented the fall of the Weimar Republic, the rise of Hitler, and the conflict in 1939. The document exercise below deals with the terms of the Treaty of Versailles and highlights the problems of the severity of the settlement and the consequences of this.

Select Bibliography

Section A

R. Henig, *Versailles and After, 1919–1933*, Methuen (1984)
L. C. B. Seaman, *From Vienna to Versailles*, Methuen (1955)
A. J. P. Taylor, *How Wars End*, Hamish Hamilton (1985)

Section B

P. Bloncourt, *The Embattled Peace, 1919–1939*, Faber and Faber (1968)
I. J. Lederer, *The Versailles Settlement: was it foredoomed to failure?*, D. C. Heath, Boston (1960)
C. L. Mee, Jnr, *The End of Order: Versailles, 1919*, Secker & Warburg (1981)
H. Nicolson, *Peacemaking, 1919*, Constable (1937)

Essays

a Were the peacemakers at Versailles inspired more by revenge than by a will to 'maintain the peace'? (ODLE Sp. Sub. 83)

b 'The Versailles Treaty was an unsatisfactory compromise between idealism and baser motives.' Discuss and comment. (UCLES Specimen 1983)

c How far did the Peace Settlements of 1919–20 embody the substance and spirit of Woodrow Wilson's Fourteen Points? (ODLE 84)

Exercise Three: Unseen

Multiple extract style. *20 marks.* *Time allowed: 45 minutes*

EXTRACT A From a meeting of the German Cabinet on 21 March 1919

Noske I still think that in extreme emergencies one fends for oneself as best one can. I cannot even recognise German guilt in Belgium. Nor in U-boat warfare either—it was a counter measure to starvation blockade. I agree that payment should be spread over a long period....

Ebert What is the extreme limit of our capacity for reparations repayments?

Rantzau Does this imply an authorisation to break off negotiations if demands endanger our very existence?

Erzberger Let us maintain, according to the Note of November 5, that reparations be limited to damage in occupied areas. No other demands should be recognised...

Rantzau I agree. The Reich reparation commission has estimated that on that basis we would have to pay 20 to 25 billions. This takes into account deliveries since armistice and perhaps colonies given up. The sum is within reason. Payments should be in kind.

Schiffer The principal consideration is what we can pay. Granting that domestic obligations and obligations towards neutrals must be met, hardly any resources are left for payment....

From: J. W. Hiden, *The Weimar Republic*, 1974

EXTRACT B Article 232 of the Treaty of Versailles, 28 June 1919

The Allied and Associated Governments recognise that the resources of Germany are not adequate, after taking into account permanent diminution of such resources which will result from other provisions of the present treaty, to make complete reparation for all such loss and damage. The Allied and Associated Governments, however, require, and Germany undertakes, that she will make compensation for all damage done to the civilian population of the Allied and Associated Powers and to their property during the period of belligerency....

EXTRACT C *The Times*, 7 May 1919

The military and naval conditions are undeniably severe, but not, in our opinion, a whit more stringent than the safety of Europe and the world requires....

The articles on reparations may not seem so satisfactory. The principle that Germany is to accept responsibility for all the loss and damage she has done appears to be accepted. At the same time we are told that the Allies recognise her inability and the inability of her confederates to make this loss and damage good....

EXTRACT D *The Evening Standard*, David Low cartoon (date unknown)

"PERHAPS IT WOULD GEE-UP BETTER IF WE LET IT TOUCH EARTH"

Cartoon supplied by permission of *The Standard*

EXTRACT E   J. M. Keynes, *Economic Consequences of the Peace*, 1920

It is evident that Germany's pre-war capacity to pay an annual foreign tribute has not been unaffected by the almost total loss of her colonies, her overseas connections, her mercantile marine, and her foreign properties,
5 by the cession of ten per cent of her territory and population, of one-third of her coal and three-quarters of her iron ore; by two million casualties among men in the prime of life; by the starvation of her people for four years; by the burden of a vast war debt; by the
10 depreciation of her currency to less than one-seventh its former value; by the disruption of her allies and their territories; by the revolution at home and Bolshevism on her borders; and by all the unmeasured ruin in strength and hope of four years of all-swallowing war
15 and final defeat.

All this, one would have supposed, is evident. Yet most estimates of a great indemnity from Germany depend on the assumption that she is in a position to conduct in the future a vastly greater trade than ever
20 she has had in the past....

Questions

a   Read Extract A.

   (i)   What plans are discussed to achieve as low a level of money repayments for Germany under reparations?   *(6)*

   (ii) What arguments are put forward for not linking guilt to payments?   *(3)*

b   Read Extracts A and B. What evidence is there in the Treaty that the Note of 5 November was ignored by the Allied governments?   *(2)*

c   What evidence is there in Extracts C and D that Britain took a more conciliatory line than some powers over German reparations?   *(5)*

d   Using Extract E:

   (i)   What does Keynes see as the Allies' greatest mistake in the estimates of how much Germany could pay?   *(2)*

   (ii) Besides those dealing with army, navy, and indemnity what other losses under the treaty, suffered by Germany, does Keynes allude to?   *(2)*

(20 marks)

Specimen answers are on p. 79.

Mussolini and Fascist Italy in the 1920s

The rise of Fascism in Italy was a direct result of the considerable problems the First World War had caused the country. As with every other combatant, Italy had expended much money, and many lives on the conflict. Her small territorial gains at the conference table did not help to solve the deeper problems of increasing state expenditure and a worsening balance of trade that saw imports taking precedence over exports. Moreover, the hopes of gaining Fiume, Dalmatia, and German colonies were false ones. The politicians who attempted to tackle these problems relied on redundant ideas. The agitation caused by social and economic distress led to the rise of some apparently powerful socialist groups, such as the Maximalists in the industrial North.

Spurred on by the Russian example, these groups tried to pressurise the Italian Government. Giolitti, the leader, seemed to give way to their demands. This invited a swift Conservative reaction, employing the strength of the Fascist Party, which was established in 1919 and led by Benito Mussolini. The Fascists lent the government the strength and ruthlessness of its *squadristi*. Hoping to manipulate this new weapon, the Italian Government allowed the Fascists to enter the election of 1921. They gained 35 seats and the all-important cloak of respectability. The subsequent rise to power of Mussolini and the Fascists was aided greatly by the divided nature of the Socialists, continuing unrest, and the ditherings of both Italian politicians and the King, Victor Emmanuel. As disorder grew, so Mussolini hatched his plot for a symbolic seizure of power in Rome, on 27 October 1922. As 14,000 Fascists marched on Rome, the Facta Government and the King chose inactivity, allowing the Fascists to enter Rome, closely followed by Mussolini, on 30 October. Slowly political power became concentrated in Mussolini's hands. New legislation, such as the Acerbo Laws on elections, ensured the majority party of almost total control in Parliament. Gradually, the powers of Prime Minister were enlarged, trade unions were broken up, and other political parties were banned. By October 1926 the Fascists were in total control and displaying all the hallmarks of a Fascist leadership: total opposition to democratic government (they accused it of corruption and incompetence); a glorification of the nation and its history; control exercised by the State; and adulation of the leader. The document exercise that follows traces the growth of Fascist control in the all-important period of the early 1920s.

Select Bibliography

Section A
M. Blinkhorn, *Mussolini and Fascist Italy*, Methuen (1984)
A. Cassels, *Fascist Italy*, Routledge & Kegan Paul (1969)
W. F. Mandle, *Fascism*, Heinemann (1968)

Section B
M. Gallo, *Mussolini's Italy*, Abelard-Schuman (1973)
D. Mack Smith, *Mussolini*, Weidenfeld & Nicolson (1982)

Essays

a Was Mussolini more than an ambitious optimist? (OCSEB 84)

b To what extent were Mussolini's foreign policies an attempt to divert the attention of Italians from economic problems? (AEB 83)

c Why was there so little opposition to Mussolini's advance to and consolidation of power during the period 1919–24? (ODLE 85)

Exercise Four: Seen

Multiple extract style.   25 marks.   Time allowed: 50 minutes

EXTRACT A   Proclamation by the Quadrumvirate, 26 October 1922

... Fascism, furthermore, does not march against the police, but against a political class both cowardly and imbecile, which in four long years has not been able to give a Government to the nation. Those who form the
5 productive class must know that Fascism wants to impose nothing more than order and discipline upon the nation and to help to raise the strength which will renew progress and prosperity....

From: A. Kersetz (ed.) *Documents in the History of the European Continent*, 1968

EXTRACT B   Part of the Fascist Programme, 1919

1. A Constituent National Assembly will proceed ... to a radical transformation of the political and economic bases of the life of the Community.

2. Proclamation of an Italian Republic. Decentralisation
5 of the Executive power ... Sovereignty of the people, exercised by universal suffrage of all citizens of the two sexes; the people retaining the initiative of referendum and veto.
3. Abolition of the Senate ...

From: A. Kersetz, ibid.

EXTRACT C   Mussolini's speech in the Chamber of Deputies, 16 November 1922

... From further communications you will know the Fascist programme in its details. I do not want, as long as I can avoid it, to rule against the Chamber; but the Chamber must feel its own position. That position
5 opens the possibility that it may be dissolved in two days or in two years. We ask full powers, because we want to assume full responsibility. Without full powers you know very well that we could not save one lira.

From: A. Kersetz, ibid.

EXTRACT D   Extracts from the Law on the Powers and Prerogatives of the Head of Government, 24 December 1925

6. No bill or motion may be submitted to either of the Houses of Parliament without the consent of the Head of the Government.
The Head of the Government has the power to
5 request that a bill, rejected by one of the House of Parliament, be voted upon again three months after the first vote....
The Head of the Government also has the power to request that a bill rejected by one of the Houses be
10 submitted to the other House to be voted upon after due examination....

From: A. Kersetz, ibid.

Questions

a With reference to Extract A:

   (i) What was the Quadrumvirate?   *(1)*

   (ii) What problems had the government faced during the, 'four long years' referred to in line 3?   *(5)*

b Which event led directly on from the Proclamation and what did Mussolini gain by it?   *(3)*

c What evidence is there in Extract C that the Fascist Programme of 1919, Extract B, is already a dead letter by 1922?   *(3)*

d What suggestion is there in Extract D that Mussolini's position between 1922 and 1925 had been precarious? How precarious had his position been?   *(5)*

(16 marks)

e Which other political law immediately followed the Powers and Prerogatives, and how did it strengthen Mussolini's position? *(4)*

f What role was played in these years by the Grand Council of Fascists and how was its character altered in 1928? *(4)*

(25 marks)

Weimar and Hitler

The Weimar Republic in Germany had an inauspicious start, coming as it did shortly after the end of the First World War, and finding itself immediately burdened with the blame for the Allies' harshness at the Treaty of Versailles. Moreover, it faced the task of paying enormous reparations bills and, at the same time, had to work under a system of proportional representation that pandered to the large number of fringe parties in German politics. Despite considerable disadvantages, the Republic survived the period of hyper-inflation, and Germany was re-established on the international scene, and the money found for the reparations bill. The lifespan of the Republic was not short, although it always seemed to be a constitution fighting for its *own* survival as well as the survival and recovery of Germany. It never endeared itself to important sections of the German community and few of these leapt to its defence when it was threatened by the growth of Nazi power. In 1933 the Republic succumbed to the Nazi threat and disappeared. The Army felt that the Republic had compromised the honour of Germany by accepting the Treaty of Versailles with its statement of war guilt. For many of the middle and property-owning classes the Republic had presided over the two worst periods of economic downturn in the country's history with the attendant loss of savings and livelihoods. Also, the ordinary people who had put up with so much felt no loyalty to the Weimar Republic. All of these antagonisms were played upon by Adolf Hitler who never shirked the responsibility of explaining exactly what the shortcomings of the Republic were to the German people. 'Fourteen years of misrule and lies' was his cry, supported by the emotive 'Stab in the back' of the Versailles settlement. Under this intense criticism the Republic began to crack. The problems brought about by the Wall Street Crash of 1929 in the USA led to the imminent collapse of the German economy and mass unemployment. All this discontent merely provided support for fringe parties, the main one being the Nazi Party. With electoral support to warrant it, Hitler forced his way into political power, intent upon the demise of the Weimar Republic. His immediate aim, an Enabling Bill, would signal the end for the Republic and he used every device he could to maximise his support in the country, including the burning of the Reichstag in the name of the Socialist and Communist parties. This and the help of the Centre Party, along with the outlawing of the Communists, gave Hitler the necessary number of votes to bring an end to the Weimar Republic. The document exercise below pinpoints the vital debates in the Reichstag on this momentous occasion.

Select Bibliography

Section A

J. W. Hiden, *The Weimar Republic*, Seminar Studies in History Series, Longman (1974)

A. Jamieson, *Adolf Hitler*, Bell & Hyman (1977)

A. J. Nicholls, *Weimar and the Rise of Hitler*, Macmillan (1979)

N. Stone, *Hitler*, Coronet (1980)

D. G. Williamson, *The Third Reich*, Seminar Studies in History Series, Longman (1982)

Section B

A. Bullock, *Hitler: A Study in Tyranny*, Penguin (1969)

J. C. Fest, *Hitler*, Penguin (1982)

J. C. G. Rohl, *From Bismarck to Hitler*, Problems and Perspectives in History Series, Longman (1970)

Essay

a Why did Hitler fail to achieve power in November 1923 but succeed in January 1933? (AEB 83)

b Why did Weimar Germany fall to the Nazis and not the Communists? (UCLES 83)

c 'Quite simply Hitler outwitted and outmanoeuvred Schleicher, Papen, and Hindenberg.' Discuss this view of the Nazis' accession to power. (OCSEB 84)

Exercise Five: Seen

Single extract style.   30 marks.   Time allowed: 60 minutes

EXTRACT A   Sir John Wheeler-Bennet, *Knaves, Fools and Heroes: Europe Between the Wars*, 1974

I shall never forget that spectacle. The Kroll Opera House, where the Reichstag met since its palace had been damaged by fire, was packed; nearly three hundred Nazi deputies, and half a hundred Nationalists; a marked
5 absence of Communists and fewer Social Democrats than could have been present, because some were in hospital, the victims of electoral violence, some had fled the country and some were just too frightened to leave their homes—and who shall blame them. The Centre
10 was a dark anxious group, unhappy and uncertain. Along the corridors of the building S.S. men, in their sinister black and silver uniforms, had been posted at intervals; their legs apart, their arms crossed, their eyes fixed and cruel, their faces otherwise expressionless,
15 looking like messengers of doom. Outside a mob of S.A. chanted threatening slogans: 'Give us the Bill or else fire and murder.' Their clamour was clearly audible within the Chamber.
        The session opened with Hitler introducing the Bill in
20 a speech remarkable for its moderation and lack of colour, but from which, we had been told, various 'fiery particles' had been deleted at the suggestion of the Foreign Ministry. He was followed by Otto Wells, leader of the Social-Democrats, who, though he seemed
25 to approach the rostrum on leaden feet, delivered a speech of such naked courage that one wanted to get up and cheer. The Government, he said, might take their lives, it could not destroy their souls. He gave his party's vote against the Bill. The effect on Hitler was
30 demonic. So infuriated was he that he gave us a second speech into which he put all the 'purple passages' which had been excised from the first, to the manifest embarrassment of von Papen and von Neurath, the Foreign Minister. His supporters were frenzied by his rhetoric;

35 again and again they rose to him; only physical and emotional exhaustion brought the Führer to a close and his followers to order. In the silence which followed, Goering called Monsignor Kaas to the tribune.
        In the party caucus, hastily summoned before the
40 opening of the session, Kaas had to admit that he had received no letter from Hitler. Brüning steadfastly and vehemently opposed support for the Bill without letter, but Kaas had wavered and had carried the Right Wing of the party with him. Now in almost breathless silence
45 he gave the Centre Party's vote in favour of the Bill.
        From my seat in the balcony I looked for Brüning and saw him refuse speech with Kaas on the latter's return to his seat. Then rising with great dignity, his head held high, he walked out of the Chamber and out
50 of the public life of Germany.

Questions

a Who was Marinus van der Lübbe and what connection did he have with the events described? *(4)*

b What part had Von Papen played in Weimar politics and why did he now find himself in league with Hitler? *(4)*

c Why might Otto Wells need, 'naked courage' (line 26) to make his speech? *(3)*

d Why was the German Parliament meeting and what would result from its activities? *(4)*

e What was the significance of Kaas' actions in the debate and vote? *(3)*

f What was:

  (i) The *'Gleichschaltung'*? *(4)*

  (ii) Operation 'Humming Bird'? *(4)*

What part did both play in Hitler's consolidation of power after 1933? *(4)*

(30 marks)

The Spanish Civil War: the bombing of Guernica

The Spanish Civil War, which broke out in 1936, was a result of a political struggle and was fought against the backdrop of economic depression, poor harvests, and unemployment. The victory of the Popular Front coalition in the elections of February 1936 invited immediate criticism and attack by the opposition Right Wing faction. The ensuing political violence which threw Spain into turmoil created the perfect conditions for politically active sections of the military, along with conservative support, to seize power.

By 17 July, a military uprising had occurred in virtually every part of Spain, but this military takeover was to be a protracted affair, throwing the country into a lengthy Civil War. The reasons for this are that the ordinary Spanish people were not willing to accept a military *fait accompli* and the army met stern resistance in all areas. Moreover, the Spanish Civil War became a symbol and battleground for foreign powers and international ideologies. As for the struggle itself, it lasted three years mainly because of the relative equality in each side's fighting strength. This is no more better shown than in the navy, where each side seized one each of the country's two battleships, the officers sympathised with the nationalist forces, and the sailors with the Republicans. In fact, the country was fairly neatly divided and a long struggle seemed very likely. Even though both Italy and Germany recognised Franco's Nationalist Government in November 1936 and gave help, the dictator's support was matched by that of the International Brigades who came to join Franco's opponents. It was the decision not to interfere in Spain's affairs taken at the League of Nations that finally prevented more help getting to the Republicans, although the European dictators, including Salazar of Portugal, did not feel bound by this agreement. Consequently, aided by the Fascist dictators, Franco slowly rolled back the Republican forces and brought an end to the Civil War in 1939. By this time the event that is dealt with by the document exercise below, the bombing of Guernica, had already happened. However, it was, according to most accounts, the result of a mission flown by a German squadron, which laid waste to the city of Guernica. This single example of the importance of foreign aid has been included because of its controversial nature and the counter-claims it has excited concerning the reasons behind the bombing and the perpetrators of the devastation itself.

Select Bibliography

Section A

R. Carr, *Modern Spain, 1875–1980*, Oxford University Press (1981)

H. Browne, *Spain's Civil War*, Seminar Studies in History Series, Longman (1983)

G. Jackson, *A Concise History of the Spanish Civil War*, Thames and Hudson (1980)

Section B

R. Fraser, *Blood of Spain: the experience of the Civil War 1936–39*, Penguin (1981)

P. Preston (ed.), *Revolution and War in Spain, 1931–1939*, Methuen (1984)

H. Thomas, *The Spanish Civil War*, Penguin (1983)

Essays

a   As a member of the International Brigade write a letter to an English newspaper explaining why you are fighting for the Republican cause in Spain. (ODLE 85)

b   Was the Spanish Civil War a struggle between Communism and Fascism? (UCLES 83)

c   Account for the outbreak of the Spanish Civil War and explain why it provoked the military and emotional responses it did from other European countries. (JMB 83)

Exercise Six: Unseen

Multiple extract style.   *25 marks.*   *Time allowed: 50 minutes*

EXTRACT A

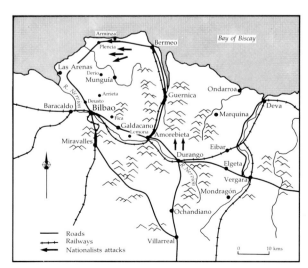

EXTRACT B   Peter Kemp, in Philip Toynbee (ed.), *The Distant Drum: Reflections on the Spanish Civil War,* 1976

After the capture of Bilbao in June 1937 there was little more fighting on that Northern Front, and I saw no more of it. I did, however, learn something about the famous Guernica controversy through my friendship
5 with a British and a French journalist who entered the town with the first Nationalist troops to occupy it, and who closely examined the damage and questioned many of the inhabitants. This was the Communists' most successful single propaganda coup of the war, and·
10 it created a myth which, fostered by the Agitprop and immortalised by the genius of Picasso, has passed into history. According to this myth Guernica was razed by German Stukas on an experiment in dive bombing. The truth is that the town, an important communications
15 centre and divisional headquarters, was bombed by the Nationalists' Air Force—not the German—who hit the railway station and an arms factory, later it was dynamited and set on fire by retreating milicianos— mostly squads of Asturian miners.

EXTRACT C   *The Times,* 28 April 1937

Guernica, the most ancient town of the Basques and the centre of their cultural tradition, was completely destroyed yesterday afternoon by insurgent raiders. The bombardment of this open town far behind the lines
5 occupied precisely three hours and a quarter, during which a powerful fleet of aeroplanes consisting of three German types, a Junkers and Heinkel bombers, and Heinkel fighters did not cease in unloading on the town bombs weighing from 1,000 lb downwards and it was
10 calculated more than 3,000 two pounder aluminium incendiary projectiles. The fighters meanwhile plunged low from above the centre of the town to machine gun those of the civilian population who had taken refuge in the fields.

EXTRACT D   J. W. D. Trythall, *Franco,* 1970

The Northern campaign opened on 31st March with Mola in command. The plan was to make the main advance ... to Bilbao, the financial and industrial centre of the region. ... The Nationalists made full use of the
5 clear skies to develop the use of air bombardment in the preparation for infantry attacks. The German and Italian airmen not only bombed the trenches, they also bombed the lines of communications, particularly with incendiary bombs which they regarded as both more
10 destructive and more frightening than ordinary explosives.
It is in this context that on 26th April, just as the

Nationalists were breaking through on the northern part of the front that the German Condor Legion
15 bombed the town of Guernica. An important centre of communication, standing at the head of a deep inlet, it was bombed for about three hours and almost destroyed. The bombardment certainly exceeded what was militarily justifiable except in so much as civilian
20 morale is a factor in war, but the Nationalists were clearly unprepared for the international cry of horror that was raised. In the following days the Nationalists' propaganda authorities issued a number of statements which demonstrated their own confusion. The central
25 point of their story was that Guernica had been destroyed by the 'Reds' as Irun had been the previous summer by petrol and dynamite. Few believed it. Germans in Spain admitted privately that bombardment had taken place and attached no further significance to
30 the fact. After all, other towns had been bombed before on a smaller but comparable scale....

EXTRACT E   *The Times,* 29 April 1937

According to a Reuter message ... insurgent headquarters at Salamanca yesterday formally and officially denied all knowledge of the raid on Guernica. It is stated that no aeroplane left Vitoria aerodrome after
5 Monday afternoon and that there was no flying at all on Tuesday. Foreign journalists at Vitoria and San Sebastian were invited to visit the aerodrome and verify these factors by inspection of the records, pilots' logbooks, petrol registers, etc. The insurgent authorities do
10 not deny that the raid on Guernica occurred but declare in the most positive way that they had no part in it.
Another message from Vitoria states that an insurgent communiqué issued there confirms the Salamanca denial that the burning of Guernica was caused by
15 insurgent bombs.

Questions

a Study Extracts A, B, and D. How far does the map extract bear out the remarks concerning Guernica's geographic and strategic position made in Extracts B and D? *(6)*

b Consult Extracts B, C, and D:

(i) What points of conflict are there concerning the raid in these extracts? *(5)*

(ii) Which of the three sources might an historian trust more than the others? Give reasons for your choice. *(6)*

(iii) Why would Extracts B and D mention the possibility of a propaganda exercise while C does not? *(2)*

c How does Extract E throw light on the assertions made in Extracts B and C about:

    (i) The part played by insurgent bombers?   *(3)*

    (ii) Sabotage in the city of Guernica?   *(3)*

(25 marks)

Austria, 1938

Hitler's desire to re-unite all German-speaking territories into a greater state that might dominate Europe was a central theme of his foreign policy. As an Austrian by birth, he also had a personal desire to bring Austria into the arms of Germany. He had tried to do exactly this in 1934 even though the joining together of Germany and Austria, the Anschluss, had been specifically forbidden by the peace treaties that followed the First World War. The Austrian Chancellor, Dollfuss, had been murdered by Austrian Nazis as a prelude to an attempted seizure of power, but this was forestalled in 1934 by the appearance of Italian troops in the Brenner Pass. Hitler backed down, uncertain of his strength and the reaction of others, notably Italy, to any violent overthrow of the Austrian Government.

By 1938 Hitler was in a stronger position, more assured of likely international reaction, and was relying on Mussolini's acquiescence to the Anschluss. As early as February 1938, the Austrian Chancellor, Von Schuschnigg, had been threatened at Berchtesgarten. Hitler wanted Austrian Nazi appointees in the Austrian Government, a general amnesty for all Austrian Nazis in detention, and other minor demands. Events then sped on, with Von Schnuschnigg preempting Hitler by declaring a plebiscite to find out whether the Austrian people wanted their independence or unification with Germany. This created the possibility of an adverse vote for Hitler and the Austrian Nazis quickly escalated tension to such a level that the referendum was postponed. Hitler then claimed Austrian prevarication and occupied the country on the strength of this so-called breach of faith. Once in control the referendum was held under German auspices and it resulted in an overwhelming majority voting for joining Germany. Certainly, there is an element of Hitler trusting to luck and relying on both Chamberlain and Mussolini to accept the *fait accompli*. There could also be truth in A. J. P. Taylor's belief that the Anschluss and Germany's invasion of Austria was a result of Hitler being taken by surprise by the quick

thinking Von Schuschnigg suddenly declaring a referendum. However, the final result was exactly what Hitler wanted and had once more confirmed his belief that he could get away with such foreign policy coups without any great criticism, let alone action, by the other Great Powers. The document exercise below outlines some of the events in this particular episode which marks one of the stages on the path to World War in 1939.

Select Bibliography

Section A

R. Henig, *Origins of the Second World War*, Methuen (1985)

Section B

W. Carr, *Arms, Autarchy, and Aggression: A Study of German Foreign Policy, 1933–1939*, Edward Arnold (1972)

K. Hildebrand, *The Foreign Policy of the Third Reich*, Batsford (1973)

A. J. P. Taylor, *Origins of the Second World War*, Penguin (1964)

E. Wiskemann, *Europe of the Dictators*, Harvester Press (1966)

Essays

a Examine the view that German policy towards Austria was governed as much by military as political considerations in the period 1931–38. (UCLES Sp. Sub. 83)

b Examine the view that it was Schuschnigg rather than Hitler who provoked the Anschluss Crisis in 1938. (ODLE Sp. Sub. 82)

c 'A welcome foreign diversion to divert attention from a potentially dangerous situation inside Germany.' Examine this view of the Anschluss of 1938. (ODLE Sp. Sub. 85)

Exercise Seven: Seen

Double extract style.   20 marks.   Time allowed: 35 minutes

EXTRACT A   Proclamation by the Austrian Chancellor, 9 March 1938

For a Free, German Austria.

People of Austria. For the first time in the history of our fatherland the leadership of the state calls for an open profession of faith in our homeland. Next Sunday,
5 March 13, is the day of the plebiscite. All of you, whatever may be your occupation or class, men and women of free Austria, you are called upon to make a profession of faith before the whole world. You are to say whether you are willing to go with us on the path
10 which we are treading, which has as its main aim social harmony and equality of rights, the final overcoming of party schisms, German peace at home and abroad, and a policy of work.

For a free and German, independent and social,
15 Christian and united Austria. For peace and work. And for equality of rights for all those who acknowledge their faith in their nation and fatherland. That is the object of my programme. To achieve this aim is our task, and the historic need of the hour....

From: A. Kersetz (ed.) Documents in the History of the European Continent, 1968

EXTRACT B   *Punch*, 22 February 1938

GOOD HUNTING

Mussolini. "All right, Adolf—I never heard a shot"

Questions

a (i) Who was the Austrian Chancellor in Extract A?
(1)

(ii) Identify the two men in Extract B. *(2)*

b What was the alternative to the Chancellor's 'path' (Extract A, lines 9–13)? *(2)*

c What is the significance of the sign 'Strictly Preserved' in the cartoon? *(4)*

d How did the plebiscite referred to in Extract A, line 5 come about? *(4)*

e What happened to the plebiscite planned for the 13 March and why did this come about? *(2)*

f Explain the succeeding events by which Germany took possession of Austria. *(5)*

(20 marks)

Hitler and the War

'I am asking of no German man more than I myself was ready to do throughout four years.' So spoke Adolf Hitler on 1 September 1939, referring to his military service in the First World War. However, by 1945, he had subjected Germany to strain, hardship, defeat, humiliation, and international condemnation. In part this was due to Hitler's own position as the director of the German war effort. Hitler's attributes as a politician, as well as his tendency for the unconventional, made him a good military leader but he excelled in short campaigns when audacity and risk-taking were invariably rewarded. In 1939, instead of stopping to consolidate his gains, he allowed himself to expand a series of localised conflicts into European, and, by implication, *world* war. Excited by the successes of the German army, confident of the other's lack of will to fight, and safe in the knowledge that a treaty secured his back against Russia, Hitler launched out on a far more risky and problematical campaign.

By May 1940 Hitler had committed Germany to a large-scale conflict and from this time continued to escalate the hostilities: firstly, against Britain in the air and then in North Africa, and secondly, with the launching of Operation Barbarossa against Russia. It was the latter that was in the end to reveal the weaknesses of Hitler's military command. He decided to keep the overall strategic picture of the war to himself and hived-off responsibilities for different areas of the conflict to the Army High Command, the OKH (*Oberkommando der Heeres*) and his own High Command of the Armed Forces, the OKW (*Oberkommando der Wehrmacht*). The contact between these two command centres was limited and did nothing to ease the problems of managing the nation's resources during the conflict. How-ever, it would be wrong to suggest that Hitler could be blamed for all the hardships that the German Army faced after 1941. Sometimes his judgement was faultless; on other occasions his plans were destroyed by the stupidity of his allies, particularly Mussolini and his ill-fated invasion of Greece (which necessitated the movement of German troops to the Balkans when they should have been prepar-ing for Russia).

1942 saw the 'beginning of the end' for Hitler. During the last years of the war his desire to take total personal control for operations increased. He was suspicious about his generals and despairing about the officers who failed to live up to his demands. By 1943, Hitler was also showing visible signs of a number of diseases, receiving continual stimul-ation and medication from drugs, and was suffering from progressively greater bouts of delusion. It is the early demonstrations of Hitler's attitudes to the control of military plans and affairs which is the theme of the document exercise that follows.

Select Bibliography

Section A

A. Jamieson, *Adolf Hitler*, Bell & Hyman (1977)

N. Stone, *Hitler*, Coronet (1980)

H. R. Trevor-Roper, *Hitler's War Directives, 1939–1945*, Pan (1966)

D. G. Williamson, *The Third Reich*, Seminar Studies in History Series, Longman (1982)

Section B

A. Bullock, *Hitler: A Study in Tyranny*, Penguin (1969)

J. C. Fest, *Hitler*, Penguin (1974)

D. Irving, *Hitler's War*, Papermac (1977)

J. Strawson, *Hitler as a Military Commander*, Batsford (1971)

Essays

a Why was Germany able to defeat so many countries so rapidly between September 1939 and the end of June 1940? (ODLE 83)

b 'Germany lost the Second World War because she needlessly attacked Russia.' Discuss this statement. (JMB 83)

c Was the invasion of Russia in 1941 the necessary consequence of Germany's policies in the 1930s? (OCSEB Sp. Sub. 81)

Exercise Eight: Unseen

Multiple extract style.   15 marks.   Time allowed: 30 minutes

EXTRACT A   Adolf Hitler's Directive for Weser Exercise, 1 March 1940

The development of the situation in Scandinavia requires the making of all preparations for the occup-ation of Denmark and Norway. This operation should prevent British encroachment on Scandinavia and the
5   Baltic. Further it should guarantee our ore base in Sweden and give our navy and the air force a wide starting line against Britain. ... In view of our military and political power in comparison with that of the Scandinavian states, the force to be employed in 'Weser
10   Exercise' will be kept as small as possible. The numerical weakness will be balanced by daring actions and surprise execution....

From: W. L. Shirer, Rise and Fall of the Third Reich, 1968

EXTRACT B   Admiral Raeder's conversation with Quisling, 11 December 1939, in Nazi naval archives

Quisling stated ... a British landing is planned in the vicinity of Stavanger and Christiansand is proposed as a possible British base. The present Norwegian Govern-ment as well as the Parliament and the whole foreign
5   policy are controlled by the well-known Jew, Hambro, a great friend of Hore-Belisha....

From: W. L. Shirer, ibid.

EXTRACT C   Alan Bullock, *Hitler: A Study in Tyranny*, 1962

From the beginning Hitler had taken a close personal interest in the Norwegian expedition. Falkenhorst was directly responsible to him and Hitler's own Command Organisation (the OKW, the Supreme Command of the
5   Armed Forces) replaced Army High Command (OKH) for the planning and direction of operations. This led to

considerable friction and departmental jealousy. More important still was the way in which it foreshadowed future developments. For Norway marks the beginning
10 of that continuous personal intervention in the daily conduct of operations which was more and more to absorb Hitler's attention and drive his generals to distraction.

EXTRACT D   Hitler's comments at a military conference, April 1941, recorded by General Halder

The war against Russia will be such that it cannot be conducted in a chivalrous fashion. This struggle is one of ideologies and racial differences and will have to be conducted with unprecedented merciless and unrelent-
5 ing harshness. All officers will have to rid themselves of obsolete ideologies. I know that the necessity for such means of waging war is beyond the comprehension of you generals but ... I insist absolutely that my orders be executed without contradiction....

From: A. Bullock, Hitler: A Study in Tyranny, *1969*

Questions

a   Study Extracts A and B.

(i) Using Extract A, give reasons for the proposed attacks in Scandinavia.   *(3)*

(ii) What part does Extract B suggest Quisling played in persuading Germany to invade Norway?   *(3)*

b   What evidence is there from Extract C that Hitler began to take power out of the army's hands?   *(2)*

c   How far are Bullock's comments in Extract C, lines 9–13, supported by the evidence in Extract D?   *(5)*

d   In Extract D, what did Hitler see as the basis of the conflict in the coming struggle between Russia and Germany?   *(2)*

(15 marks)

Stalin and party leadership

After Lenin's death in 1924, the leadership of the Russian people was very much undecided. In his own 'Testament', Lenin had foreseen the problems that might be caused by a struggle for leadership and certainly was worried by a likely confrontation between Trotsky and Stalin. Lenin's prediction proved correct, but it was Stalin who slowly garnered the trappings of leadership, and finally established the so-called 'cult of personality'. Until he was denounced by Krushchev in 1956, three years after his death, Stalin's influence was still very strong.

Stalin's drive to power was relentless, ruthless and cunning. He was fortunate to have occupied important positions after the Revolution of 1917, firstly as Commissar for Nationalities and later as a member of both the Political and Organisational Bureaux. By 1922 he was also General Secretary of the Party. After Lenin's death, Stalin could start to manipulate both friends and opponents. He cleverly used Kamenev and Zinoviev to oust Trotsky from the left-wing of the party, exluding him totally in 1927 and exiling him in 1928. With Trotsky on the way out, Stalin turned to the right-wing of the party, and particularly Bukharin, to help him reduce the power of the left. Both Kamenev and Zinoviev were victims of this *volte face.* Able now to

concentrate on the right, Stalin forced Bukharin to acknowledge publicly the error of his ways in 1929.

By 1929 Stalin was dominant. He could never relax, always wary of potential opponents and rivals and kept Russia and its politicians under rigid control for the rest of his life. For instance, his power was such that no party conferences were held between 1936 and 1952, and considering the changes that Stalin made and the ways he went about them, not giving his potential rivals a political forum to air their grievances was a sensible move. It was during this period that Russia was forced to change her ways, undergo massive industrialisation, suffer great agricultural unrest, and pay dearly for the drive towards modernisation. Such were the costs, both material and human, that Stalin's need for control became even more necessary. After his death he was roundly criticized for the way in which his personal rule overshadowed the idea of collective leadership. However, the passing of time has seen a mellowing of views and some Russians have come to believe that Stalin was a necessary evil without whom Russia would have floundered. Others, and many Western commentators, prefer to retain the image of the ruthless politician and monstrous tyrant with blood on his hands.

These conflicting views are alluded to in the document exercise that follows which concentrates on the Stalin leadership debate.

Select Bibliography

Section A

M. McCauley, *Stalin and Stalinism*, Seminar Studies in History Series, Longman (1983)

V. Serge, *From Lenin to Stalin*, Monad Press, New York (1973)

Section B

R. Conquest, *The Great Terror*, Penguin (1971)

I. Deutscher, *Stalin*, Penguin (1966)

A. B. Ulam, *Stalin: The Man and his Era*, Allen Lane (1974)

Essays

a Consider the statement that 'Stalin's character in the last seven years of his life underwent a deterioration.' (AEB Sp. Sub. 82)

b Did the death of Stalin result in any significant changes in Russia's domestic and foreign policies? (ODLE 83)

c Account for the failure of collective leadership in the Soviet Union in the period 1953–64. (UCLES 83)

Exercise Nine: Unseen

Multiple extract style.   20 Marks.   Time allowed: 45 minutes

EXTRACT A Speech by Comrade D. A. Lazurkina (party member since 1902) at the 22nd Congress, October 1961

Comrade delegates—I wholly and fully support the proposals of Comrade Spiridonov and other comrades who have spoken here on removing Stalin's body from the Lenin Mausoleum.

5   In the days of my youth I began my work under the leadership of Vladimir Ilyich Lenin, learned from him and carried out his instructions. . . . And then comrades, in 1937 I was to share the lot of many. I had an executive post in the Leningrad Province Party

10   Committee and, of course, was also arrested. When they arrested me and when the prison doors closed behind me, I felt such a horror, not for myself but for the Party. I could not understand why old Bolsheviks were being arrested. Why? This 'why?' was so agoniz-

15   ing, so incomprehensible. . . . And then I returned completely rehabilitated. I arrived just at the time when the 20th Party Congress was in session. This was the first time I learned the hard truth about Stalin. And now at the 22nd Congress as I hear about the disclosed evil

20   deeds and crimes that were committed in the Party with Stalin's knowledge, I wholly and fully endorse the proposal for the removal of Stalin's remains from the Mausoleum.

     The great evil caused by Stalin consists not only in

25   the fact that many of our best people perished, not only in the fact that arbitrary actions were committed and innocent people were shot and imprisoned without trial. This was not all. The entire atmosphere that was created in the Party at that time was totally at variance

30   with the spirit of Lenin . . .

From: T. Riha (ed.) Readings in Russian Civilisation, Volume III, 1964

EXTRACT B R. N. Carew Hunt, *A Guide to Communist Jargon*, 1957

The cult of the personality is the euphemism employed today for Stalin's crimes and blunders, or at least those which his successors, albeit involved in them, have found it convenient to disown. But before examining it

5   in this particular connection it should be noted that it has a wider extension, as it is an expression of the view that history is made by so-called 'great men' this being opposed to the classical Marxist doctrine which teaches that it develops according to a prescribed pattern

10 determined by economic laws. . . .

    The attack on the cult of personality, as reflected in Stalin's autocratic rule and in the repeated assertions that he was supreme in every field of creative activity, gathered impetus after the Twentieth Congress, and

15 was taken up by one Soviet journal after another in order to show its baneful effects in the particular field in which the journal in question had an interest. An unsigned article of exceptional violence in *Young Communist* of February 1956 declared that it had led to

20 the complete suppression of the Komsomol as an independent organisation; *Questions of Philosophy* of April complained that it had had the effect of limiting study of the problems of dialectical and historical materialism to those which Stalin had dealt with in his

25 writing devoted to this subject, and to a consequent neglect of the works of Marx, Engels and Lenin; while *Soviet Pedagogics* of September dwelt upon its malign influence on the young, observing *inter alia* that the introduction of compulsory elementary education had

30 been represented as due to Stalin's 'fatherly solicitude', whereas it had in fact been rendered necessary by the development of Soviet society. . . .

EXTRACT C *Pravda*, May 1953

One of the fundamentals of party leadership is collectivity in deciding all important problems of party work. It is impossible to provide genuine leadership if inner party democracy is violated in the party organisation, if

5 genuine collective leadership and widely developed criticism and self-criticism are lacking. Collectiveness and the collegium principle represent a very great force in party leadership....

The principle of collectivity in work means, above all,
10 that decisions adopted by the party committees on all cardinal questions are the fruit of collective discussion. No matter how experienced leaders may be, no matter what their knowledge and ability, they do not possess

and they cannot replace the initiative and experience of
15 a whole collective....

Individual decisions are always or almost always one sided decisions. Hence the very important requirements that decisions must rest on the experience of many and must be the fruit of collective effort. If this is not so, if
20 decisions are adopted individually serious errors can occur in work....

EXTRACT D

The Evening Standard,
David Low cartoon
(date unknown)

Cartoon supplied by
permission of
The Standard

"IT'S QUEER HOW YOU REMIND ME OF SOMEONE, JOSEF . . ."

EXTRACT E   Adam B. Ulam, *Stalin: The Man and his Era*, 1974

Only the most fatuous moralist will deny that Stalinism is an example of an oppressive social system which in terms of its own premises worked. Some of the most horrifying tales of Stalin's time bear witness to that
5 uncomfortable truth. There is no political opposition or alienation in Ivan Denisovich's camp ... Nadezhda Mandelstam's gripping book about her poet husband, martyred for writing a few irreverent verses about Stalin (which he read just to a few closest friends, at
10 least one of whom denounced him). ... But the writings of Osip Mandelstam, who died, probably demented, in a forced labour camp in 1938 or 1939, are still proscribed in the Soviet Union, and any criticism of Joseph Stalin must again be temperate and balanced by
15 recognition of his great services to the party and state. Any critique of the Stalin system that enumerates cruelties—and it could never be complete or vivid enough—encounters the obvious rebuttal: Why, then, could such a society not only survive, but defeat a
20 powerful foreign enemy, create a mighty industrial base, and become an object of worldwide emulation and of the loyalties of millions living in countries where no such atrocities were being perpetrated?

Questions

a   Consult Extracts A and B.

  (i) What evidence is there in Extract A to support the contention that a police state existed in Russia in Stalin's time? *(4)*

  (ii) How does Extract B suggest that Stalin's power during the 'cult of personality' went beyond mere police control? *(4)*

b   Consult Extracts C and D.

  (i) How does Extract C explain the weakness of Soviet government during Stalin's 'cult of personality'? *(4)*

  (ii) How does Low in his cartoon portray fears about the 'cult of personality'? *(2)*

c   Read Extract E.

  (ii) How does this extract help to substantiate the descriptions of Stalin's Russia given in Extract A? *(2)*

  (ii) How does Ulam justify Stalin's use of his power in Russia? *(4)*

(20 marks)

Specimen answers: Russia 1905–06

a The general grievance in the workers' petition is that they feel excluded by their economic and political masters. They demand fair wages and treatment, including medical provision at work. On a more abstract level, they ask for truth and justice. Interference from officialdom and the lack of opportunity to speak their minds freely feature highly on their list of grievances. An over-active bureaucracy is blamed for the evils inside Russia which are also seen as unfortunate consequences of a 'shameful war'. These specific grievances are all subsumed in a general plea for political representation based on a Constituent Assembly elected by universal suffrage.

b (i) Lenin suggests that the government was perfectly happy for the strike movement in Russia to grow, at least initially. The government felt that as strike activity increased, so it would be easier for it to justify massive repression. The growth of strike action also gave Tsardom the opportunity to hit out at the largest possible number of its 'enemies' who would reveal themselves as discontent grew.

(ii) However, far from killing off the revolutionary movement, repression was fanning its flames and making it more difficult to control. When its attempts at repression failed, the government had no alternative but to try to 'buy off' the revolutionaries with belated concessions such as the granting of a nine-hour working day.

c Milyukov states that any suggestion that the revolutionary movement is the work of a few 'hot-heads' is criminal in its misinterpretation of the serious and deteriorating situation in Russia in 1905. Such is the level of agitation that the government cannot even 'buy off' the revolutionaries and any attempts to do so merely increase the level of discontent. Moreover, those classes of the population who would normally not become involved in such activities were openly contemplating joining the opponents of Tsardom. As usually law-abiding people began to criticize the government, Milyukov discerns a fundamental shift in the broadening of the base and appeal of the revolutionary forces.

d (i) The Tsar and Witte discussed two possible solutions in 1905. The first relied upon repression and an attempt to 'crush' the rebellion but, as the Tsar admits, this would probably have given a respite rather than a solution to the problem. The second option relied upon giving in gracefully to the rebels by granting a Constitution that satisfied their demands.

(ii) All three authors seem to be in agreement about the likely outcomes of the two possible options open to the government. Lenin categorically states that the rebels will not give in, nor will they be defeated by force or be bought off by economic concessions. Their demands are for political concessions and this will necessitate the granting of a Constitution. Similarly, Milyukov suggests that the rebels have grown too strong and are too committed to their ideals to be 'bought-off' or frightened into extinction by repression. They might not be strong enough to overthrow the Tsar but their continued opposition will ensure that the Tsar can no longer govern. Like Lenin, Milyukov sees the only solution to be for the government to pursue a path that does not lead to either 'palliatives' or repression—leaving the granting of a Constitution as the most likely alternative. Looking at the events of 1905 from another viewpoint, the Tsar and Witte come to similar conclusions: however unpleasant it may be the solution seems to involve the granting of a Constitution. Nicholas rejects the idea of repression, echoing the thoughts of Milyukov in particular, realising that this will bring only temporary respite. Once repression has been conceded the Tsar has only one option open to him. Hence, all three authors are in accord in their appraisals of the events and likelihood of success, or failure, of potential solutions to Russia's problems in 1905.

Specimen answers: The Treaty of Versailles

a (i) The German Cabinet explore a number of possibilities in their attempts to limit Germany's money repayments under the reparations clauses of the Treaty of Versailles. The first suggestion from Noske is that the payments be spread over a long period hoping to lessen the burden and diminish the scale of the payments as the years pass. Rantzau offers a second possibility of using the ploy of breaking off negotiations totally if the reparations demands are too high. Thirdly, Erzberger believes that reparations should be limited to 'damage in occupied areas'. Fourthly, Rantzau floats the idea of making payments in kind, suggesting the use of colonies and materials, in order to minimise the amount of money involved in debt repayments.

(ii) The cabinet has strong feelings on the question of guilt in the hostilities. Noske on the one hand, simply refuses to accept that any guilt was involved in Germany's dealings with Belgium. On the other hand he gives Germany's understandable desire to break the 'starvation blockade' as his reason for the U-boat campaign and can accept no guilt in this instance. Noske gains support from Erzberger who also wishes to discuss guilt in terms of the military hostilities only and insists that guilt in general is different to Germany's guilt for damages in 'occupied areas' for which she should expect to pay.

b The Allied governments are at pains to make absolutely clear in the Treaty of Versailles that Germany will compensate the injured parties for 'all damage done'. Hence, the German Cabinet's note of 5 November referred to in Extract A, which asked for liability to be limited to damage 'in occupied areas' seems to have been totally ignored in the Allied governments final decision about reparations.

c *The Times* extract, C, does not present an official view of the Treaty of Versailles but it is an informed view presented on a national level. The journalist admits the severity of the Treaty agreements especially in the military and naval fields but finds these, at least, understandable. However, he goes on to highlight the basic contradiction of the articles on reparations. Germany certainly admits guilt and agrees to responsibility

but the Allies, knowing full well Germany's inability to pay, still insists that she does so. Similarly, the cartoon, Extract D, shows Germany's indemnity burden to be far too great for her weakened state but it is Briand and not the undecided looking Lloyd George who is using the whip and taking the more unbending and rigid stand over reparations.

d (i) Keynes is very forthright in his views in Extract E. He sees the Allies' greatest mistake as being the simple belief that a beaten and demoralised power, Germany, can achieve a higher level of economic activity after defeat in the war than she could ever hope to achieve in the period before the war without all the deprivations of defeat and the loss of her economic life blood.

(ii) Keynes highlights the extent of Germany's losses as a result of the Treaty. These include their colonies and foreign properties, loss of populations and mineral wealth, the degeneration of her people, the loss of her work-force, and general economic decline that was creating a situation of political instability.

Undirected gobbets

As mentioned in the introduction to this section, sometimes you may be presented with a number of gobbets and asked to select three or four and comment on them. It is important to adopt a strategy for dealing with these.

Firstly, it is important to read all the extracts through, because, unlike a multi-sourced exercise, you will have to select the gobbets that suit you and your knowledge best. In any case gobbets in exercises such as these tend to be a few lines at the most. Only select those gobbets you fully understand and that raise questions about which you have some detailed information. There is no surer way of displaying ignorance or misunderstanding than choosing gobbets to write about which raise unfamiliar points. Having selected the required number of gobbets it is best to approach them using the following checklist:

1 Identify the extract if known, or required. Certainly, be sure to check the source of the extract making a special note of the author (speaker, etc.), the circumstances (Prison, Parliament, etc.), and the date.

2 If it is relevant, explain the importance of the larger document from which the gobbet is taken.

3 Explain the background to the particular point being raised by the gobbet.

4 Specify the exact point, or points, raised by the gobbet.

5 If known, or required, mention any other relevant points raised by the document from which the gobbet is taken.

6 Briefly conclude with a little of the subsequent history of the topic concentrating on the effects of the point, or points, raised by the gobbet.

Whether you use all six of these points on the check-list will depend very much on the type of gobbet question you encounter. If the gobbets are a selection from collections of documents you have studied and are expected to be familiar with, then points one, two, and five will require evidence of your knowledge. If the gobbets are totally unseen, in that you may not have come across them before, then the exercise will be designed to test your factual knowledge and not that of the sources. Whatever the style, the golden rules remain the same:

● Do not use more than the time allowed

● Remember that the marks will be split equally for each gobbet comment that you make

● Remember that, whatever the number of gobbets for comment, if this question replaces an essay then a similar amount of writing will be required (although if anything you will tend to write a little less)

Having outlined the plan of attack there follows an example of a gobbet and answer:

> This appeal raises the question whether trade unions can lawfully apply any of their funds in promoting the election, paying the election expenses, and providing for the maintenance of a Member of Parliament. . . .
>
> Lord Justice Farwell, *The Osborne Judgment*, 1909

Checklist point A reply to the request to comment on this extract might be:

[1] These are the words of Lord Justice Farwell, one of the judges who heard the case put by Osborne, on appeal, in December 1909. His words had far-reaching consequences

[2] for both the trade unions and the Labour Movement. He was judging the issue brought to the courts originally in 1908 by W. V. Osborne, Walthamstow Branch

[3] Secretary of the Railway Servants. It had been the practice of trades unions to levy their members for funds to use to support Labour MPs who relied on contributions. However, Osborne was a Liberal supporter and he objected to the blanket use of political levies for Labour Party upkeep. He based his case on the contention that although previous trade union legislation did not bar unions from such actions, neither did they condone them.

[4] Osborne took the issue to the High Court in 1908 and was unsuccessful. However, on appeal this decision was overturned. Moreover, on going to the Lords, Osborne's complaint was upheld and an injunction was granted restraining the Railway Servants from raising a political levy and from giving much-needed help to

[5] Labour MPs. Although, for specific reasons, the Lords' judgments varied—from stating that political levies were not a legitimate field of activity for trade unions, to rejecting the implication that the Labour Party was the only one capable of protecting the interests of the working man—the general conclusion was the same.

[6] The judgment of 1909 was a hard blow for unions and Labour Party alike. In 1911 the lot of the Labour Party was improved by an Act providing for the payment of MPs. Despite this, the trade unions continued to agitate for a reappraisal of the

Osborne Judgment. Their endeavours were unrewarded until 1913. This was mainly because there was great pressure on Parliamentary time, as a result of Liberal reforming legislation. However, in 1913 the Trade Union Act improved matters by allowing Unions to raise levies, as long as these were placed in separate funds, and also provided that those wishing to do so could opt out of payment, and that a ballot of members decided where the funds went.

For the purpose of practice in this type of question there follow some examples of gobbets on the First World War and the British Welfare State.

The First World War

Comment on *four* of the following:

EXTRACT A   28 June 1914

From: BBC Hulton Picture Library

EXTRACT B   Command from Kaiser Wilhelm II to General Von Kluck
It is my Royal and Imperial command that you ... exterminate first the treacherous English, and walk over General French's contemptible little army.

EXTRACT C   Grand Admiral von Tirpitz, *My Memoirs*
The decision of the war turns exclusively on whether Germany or England can hold out the longer. It is absolutely necessary to occupy Calais and Boulogne.

EXTRACT D   Rear-Admiral Paul Schlieper
5 In the submarine Germany has an advantage which must be used with all determination.

EXTRACT E   Crown Prince William of Germany, *My War Experiences*
The mighty drive for the battles for Verdun in 1916 was at an end. ... Small wonder if this ill-starred end to our efforts wrung the hearts of the responsible commanders.

EXTRACT F   Admiral Jellicoe, quoted in G. Bennett, *The Battle of Jutland*, 1964

10 If in endeavouring to destroy the German Fleet we run risks which may prejudice our success in the greater object of destruction of Germany, those risks are too great.

EXTRACT G   President Woodrow Wilson, 2 April, 1917

We have no selfish ends to serve. We desire no conquest, no domination. We seek no indemnities for ourselves, no material compensation for the sacrifices we shall freely make.

EXTRACT H   Johannes Spiess, a German U-boat Commander, in *Sechs Jahre U-Boat Fahrten*

Every ten minutes the convoy changed course by about twenty degrees behind its
15 leader. Four escort vessels, fanned out before the convoy, provided it with light, and two destroyers were zigzagging on both sides.

EXTRACT I   Erich von Ludendorff, *Ludendorff's Own Story*

Early on August 8th, in dense fog ... they penetrated deep into our positions ...

EXTRACT J   L. G. Morrison, *The Eighth of August*, 1918

Four hundred tanks in line of battle. Good going, firm ground, wheel to wheel, and blazing, brilliant weather ....

EXTRACT K   D. Lloyd George, *War Memoirs*, 1933

20 Word was telegraphed (from Germany) back to the Forest of Compiegne authorising Erzberger and his colleagues to sign the Armistice. They did so at 5 a.m. on November 11th, and at 11.00 a.m., the cannon-fire ceased along the battle front ...

The British Welfare State and Nationalism

Comment on *four* of the following:

EXTRACT A   *The Evening Standard*, David Low cartoon (date unknown)

RIGHT TURN

Cartoon supplied by permission of *The Standard*

EXTRACT B White Paper on Social Insurance, September, 1944. (CMD. 6550)
... a nation with a high power of production would not have solved its problem if it
included any appreciable section of people who were in want, whether through loss of
individual earning power, due to ill-health, unemployment or old age, or through
inability to provide properly for their children. Only when this problem is also solved
5 has a community achieved genuine social security.

EXTRACT C Brief of the Reid Committee, September, 1944
to examine the present technique of coal production from face to wagon, and to advise
what technical changes are necessary in order to bring the Industry to a state of full
technical efficiency.

EXTRACT D *The Times*, 27 July, 1945
British History affords no such example of the reversal of national leadership on the
10 morrow of a crowning victory.

EXTRACT E Clement Attlee, 12 November, 1946. Parliamentary Debates
5/cdxxx/p. 35
First ... is electricity supply. Here we shall complete some of the work begun in
1926 ...

EXTRACT F National Health Act, 1946
The services so provided shall be free of charge except where any provision of this Act
expressly provides for the making and recovery of charges.

EXTRACT G Bank of England Act, 1946
15 ... to bring the capital stock of the Bank of England into public ownership and bring
the bank under public control ...

EXTRACT H Mr Silkin, House of Commons speech, 29 January, 1947
... The objects of town and country planning are being increasingly understood and
accepted. ... More than ever, there is today heavy pressure on our limited supply of
land. ...

EXTRACT I The Transport Act, 1947
20 ... to provide and promote an efficient, adequate, economical and properly integrated
system of public inland transport and port facilities within Great Britain for passengers
and goods.

Section Three: Examination Boards' Examples

The exercises which follow are all taken from examination papers set by various boards over the past few years, although examples given in specimen papers are also used. Topics selected are those central to a study of twentieth century history, both British and European, that have not already appeared in Section Two. The only changes made to the papers are in the headings and these are the same as those used in Section Two, giving information on the style of question, mark allocation, and time allowed to complete the exercise. The line numbering of extracts, either starting at 5 on each extract or continuing through all extracts, follows the style of individual boards.

British

The Liberal Budget: 1909	JMB 1981
Wartime coalition	UL 1982
The Labour Government and the Welfare State	UL 1982

European

Revolution in Russia, 1914–33	AEB Specimen 1987
Origins of the Second World War	UCLES Specimen 1983
The German problem and the peace of Europe	UL 1984

The Liberal Budget 1909: Unseen

Joint Matriculation Board 1981

Multiple extract style. 25 marks. Time allowed: 45 minutes

Read Extracts A, B, C, D and E which are printed on a separate sheet, and then, **using only the evidence they contain**, answer the following questions:

Questions

a Consult Extracts A and B.
What were the aims of the Liberals in proposing the budget in 1909? How did their proposals seek to realise these aims? *(9)*

b Consult Extracts A, B and E.
Show why Philip Snowden (Extract E) could argue that 'This budget ... applies the Socialist idea that taxation should appropriate socially created wealth.' *(4)*

c Consult Extracts C and D.
Analyse the basis of Conservative opposition to the 1909 budget indicated in these extracts. *(6)*

d Consult Extracts D and E.
Explain the major differences between Conservatism and Socialism as indicated in these two extracts. *(6)*

———
25
———

EXTRACT A   Lloyd George, Speech at Limehouse, East London, 30 July 1909

It is rather a shame that a rich country like ours—probably the richest in the world, if not the richest the world has ever seen—should allow those who have toiled all their days to end in penury and possibly
5 starvation. It is rather hard that an old workman should have to find his way to the gates of the tomb, bleeding and footsore, through the brambles and thorns of poverty. We cut a new path for him—an easier one, a pleasanter one, through fields of waving corn. We are
10 raising money to pay for the new road—aye, and to widen it so that 200,000 paupers shall be able to join in the march. There are many in the country blessed by Providence with great wealth, and if there are amongst them men who grudge out of their riches a fair
15 contribution towards the less fortunate of their fellow countrymen they are very shabby rich men.
   We propose to do more by means of the Budget. We
are raising money to provide against the evils and the sufferings that follow from unemployment. We are
20 raising money for the purpose of assisting our great friendly societies to provide for the sick and the widows and orphans. We are providing money to enable us to develop the resources of our own land. I do not believe any fair-minded man would challenge
25 the justice and the fairness of the objects which we have in view in raising this money.

EXTRACT B   Winston Churchill, Speech at Preston, 3 December 1909

You are now familiar with the actual proposals of the Budget. There was the income tax somewhat increased, but also diminished for the poorest of income-tax payers. There was the super-tax which is to press so
5 heavily upon those who have over £5,000 a year.—(Laughter.) There were the estate, legacy, and stamp duties, there was the tax on motors, which, after all, exact their own tax from the good nature of the public who don't use those conveyances—(laughter),—there
10 was the tax on motors which was largely used for improving the roads to aid the motoring public and at the same time improve the roads and development of the country, there was the tax upon tobacco and the tax upon whisky which we put on deliberately with a view
15 to making sure that it should not be said that we had been afraid of asking the working man for his share—(cheers),—which, indeed, he had shown himself quite ready to pay—(cheers)—in a manly and dignified fashion. There were the taxes on liquor licences which
20 we regard as a gift from the State and a very valuable property which the State has allowed to pass from its hands at a wholly inadequate rental, there were the three taxes on land—the revenue tax and the increment duty and the tax on undeveloped land—which consti-
25 tute the first attempt to secure for the great population who make the wealth and create the land value of this small island some share in the communal values which arise from their exertions.—(Cheers.) Then there was the tax on mining royalties—(cheers),—again a tax not
30 levied on industry or on any reproductive process, not levied on anything which makes for the wealth of its owner at the same time as it makes for the wealth of other people and the wealth of the world in general, but levied on a private tax, a share of a private tax taken
35 and properly taken to sustain the revenues of the State and of the whole community. Broadly that was the

Budget which we have produced, which the Lords have
destroyed, and which we still propose.——(Loud and
prolonged cheers.)

40 This Budget has caused no shock to credit——(hear,
hear),—no dislocation of business, no setback to the
trade revival. It imposes no burdens on the necessaries
of life, it imposes no extra burdens on the comforts of
life, it interposes no impediment in the way of enter-
45 prise or trade. Nothing in it makes it harder for the
labouring man to maintain that physical strength which
is the prop of his household and his home.–(Hear, hear.)
Nothing in the Budget made it harder for the industri-
ous fellow whether he worked with his head or his
50 hands to keep a home together in decent comfort.
Nothing made it impossible for the middle-class citizen
to maintain his style and status of living, and I tell you
that nothing in it would have affected in any sensible
degree the happiness or even the style of the wealthier
55 classes in this country.

EXTRACT C   Austen Chamberlain, Speech in London,
19 May 1909

The great mass of those who will be hit by these taxes
nominally placed upon the idle rich are men who in
their own spheres are discharging their full share of
public duty as well as carrying on in the country or in
5 the towns the life and industry which is necessary to
our national prosperity. In my opinion the cumulative
effect of the different taxes proposed in the Budget
would be to work in the course of years, and in no too
distant time, a revolution in our country life which will
10 hit first and foremost of course, which will strike
directly, the well-to-do, but which will, glancing from
their shoulders, fall with added weight upon those of
the poor and the labouring classes.

EXTRACT D   Hugh Cecil, *Conservatism*, 1912

There is no antithesis between Conservatism and
Socialism, or even between Conservatism and Liberal-
ism. Subject to the counsels of prudence and to a
preference for what exists and has been tried over the
5 unknown, Conservatives have no difficulty in welcom-
ing the social activity of the State. The point which
principally distinguishes their attitude from that of other
political parties is a rigorous adherence to justice. This
involves resistance to any measure which would
10 impoverish classes or individuals by depriving them of
all or even of a considerable fraction of what they
possess. It is so plain that to take what one man has and
give it to another is unjust, even though the first man
be rich and the second poor, that it is surprising that
15 legislative measures which consist essentially in such
transfers should ever be advocated or defended. ... To
carry out . ... the enrichment of the poor by impover-
ishment of the rich, even if it were practically an
efficient policy, would not be just. But in fact, such a
20 measure would be as unworkable as it is immoral. The
apprehension of confiscation would oblige people to
export or to conceal their wealth, and the uncertainty
whether the accumulations of wealth in the future
would be respected, would be fatal to the enterprise and
25 confidence that enable commerce and industry to
prosper.

EXTRACT E   'The Budget', *Socialist Review* (article by
Philip Snowden), 1909

The purpose of Socialism being to get social wealth for
social use, it follows that any proposal which will secure
some portion of social wealth for social use is in accord
with Socialist principles. There are two ways by which
5 that purpose can be pursued: by transferring particular
industries or services to the public, and by taking, by
taxation, portions of the social wealth which individuals
appropriate as rent, interest, and profit....

This budget ... to a greater extent than any former
10 Budget, applies the Socialist idea that taxation should
appropriate socially created wealth. ... This is the
feature of the Budget which justifies Socialist support.

Wartime coalition: Seen

University of London 1982

Single extract style.   31 marks.   Time allowed: 60 minutes

Study the extract below and then answer questions **a** to **f** which follow:

David Lloyd George to a Labour Party delegation,
7 December 1916

Delay in war is as fatal as in an illness .... Action which today may save the life of a country taken a week late is too late. I thought, rightly or wrongly, that there was delay, hesitation and vacillation, and that we were not
5 waging this war with the determination, promptitude and relentlessness—let us make no mistake about it— with which it must be waged. We cannot send men to carnage without seeing that at any rate everything is being done to give them a fair chance to win through
10 to victory. They are prepared to make the sacrifice, and we, on the other hand, must support them with all the strength and all the will with which we are endowed. So it was I made certain proposals. I do not believe any Prime Minister, whoever he is, if he has the
15 strength of a giant mentally and physically and morally, can possibly undertake the task of running Parliament and running the war. That is the conviction I have received. I am still of the same opinion, and I shall certainly act upon it if I form an Administration.
20 Whoever undertakes to run the War must put his whole strength into it and he must make other arrangements with regard to Parliament ....

It is obvious that no Government can be carried on in this country, whether during war or peace, without, I
25 won't say the support of Labour, but the co-operation of Labour. Upon its determination to help in winning this War, everything depends, and therefore I invited you here, through Mr. Henderson, who has been my colleague for eighteen months or two years, and let
30 me say at once that I never want a more loyal col- league. He has faced tasks which I thought were difficult, but which were twice as difficult for him because of his association with Labour .... I invited him to communicate with the leaders of Labour in this
35 country with a view to inviting their co-operation in the Government of the country—not in a subordinate position, but a real share in the War Committee, to direct the War; a real share in the Administration by those who are not members of the War Committee,
40 because those members of the War Committee ought on the whole to be free from the burdens of depart- mental work ....

I have given you very fairly and very frankly my own views of the only way in which this War has got to be
45 won. If it is a national War, everyone must contribute, and it is on that basis alone we shall be able to achieve a great triumph.

Questions

(Maximum marks)
[as indicated]

a Who was 'Mr Henderson' (line 28), and in what circumstances had he been Lloyd George's 'colleague' for 'eighteen months or two years' (line 29)?   *(3)*

b What evidence supported Lloyd George's view that there had been 'delay, hesitation and vacillation' (line 4) in the waging of the war up to the point at which he was speaking?   *(5)*

c Explain how the 'proposals' (line 13) which Lloyd George had made led to the situation in which he was trying to 'form an Administration' (line 19).   *(6)*

d Why was Lloyd George insistent that 'everything' depended on 'the determination' of organised Labour to 'help in winning this War' (lines 26–27)?   *(5)*

e What evidence does the extract provide to suggest that winning the co-operation of the Labour Party was not an easy task?   *(4)*

f How far may the evidence contained in this extract be used in an assessment of Lloyd George's qualities as a politician both in war and in the subsequent peace?
(8)

The Labour Government and the Welfare State, 1945–51: Seen

University of London 1982

Double extract style.   31 marks.   Time allowed: 60 minutes

Study Extracts I and II below and then answers questions **a** to **f** which follow:

EXTRACT I   C. R. Atlee, *As It Happened*, 1954

We realised that the application of socialist principles in a country such as Britain with a peculiar economic structure based on international trade required great flexibility.

5 We were also well aware of the especially difficult situation of the country resulting from the great life-and-death struggle from which we had emerged victorious. But, in our view, this did not make change in the socialist direction less necessary. On the contrary, it
10 was clear that there could be no return to past conditions. The old pattern was worn out and it was for us to weave the new. Thus, the kind of reproach levelled at us by Churchill, that, instead of uniting the country by a programme of social reform on the lines of
15 the Beveridge Report, we were following a course dictated by social prejudice or theory, left us completely unmoved. We had not been elected to try to patch up an old system but to make something new. Our policy was not a reformed capitalism but progress towards a
20 democratic socialism.

In fact, during these years a peaceful revolution has taken place. Broadly speaking, there has been a great levelling-up of conditions. The great mass of abject poverty has disappeared. Full employment and the
25 development of the social services are, of course, the principal factors in this.

EXTRACT II   J. Saville, *The Welfare State: an Historical Approach*, 1957

A main reason why public opinion in general, and the Labour movement in particular, have become confused as to the essentially bourgeois nature of the Welfare
30 State is that both in the propaganda of the Labour Party and in the criticisms of its opponents, the legislation of the 1945 Labour Government was labelled 'socialist'.

The melancholy business of making a collection of the idiotic and wildly unrealistic statements of Labour's
35 intellectual leaders concerning the 'social revolution' of the post-war years must be left to others; but it must be noted that given the attribution of 'socialist' to the measures of nationalization and 'free' social security benefits, even the rank and file of the Labour movement
40 began to believe this propaganda which came as much from those who purport to be its friends as from its enemies ....

As for the claim that the ... Welfare State is an early form of a socialist society, it must be emphasized that
45 both in Western Europe and the United States social security schemes are placed firmly within the framework of a free enterprise economy and no one suggests that what is a natural development within a mature capitalist economy should be given new names.

Questions   *(Maximum marks)*
                                                    [as indicated]

a (i) Explain the reference to 'the Beveridge Report' (line 15).
   (ii) What is meant by 'bourgeois' (line 29)?
   (iii) What position did Churchill occupy when making the 'reproach' referred to in line 12?   *(3)*

b Both writers, one a politician and one an academic, claimed to be socialists. What do you deduce about their definitions of socialism from these Extracts? *(4)*

e What constraints were imposed upon the Labour Government by Britain's 'peculiar economic structure' and by its emergence from the 'great life-and-death struggle' (lines 6 and 7)?   *(4)*

d What elements of Attlee's social and economic policy contributed most to the 'great levelling-up of conditions' and the disappearance of 'the great mass of abject poverty' (lines 23–24)?   *(6)*

e '... Progress toward a democratic socialism' (line 19–20)?
   '... a natural development within a mature capitalist economy' (line 48–49); which seems to you a fairer description of the Welfare State?   *(6)*

f Discuss Attlee's claim that during these years 'a peaceful revolution' (line 21) took place, in the light of the charge that there have been 'idiotic and wildly unrealistic statements about the "social revolution" of the post-war years' (lines 34–36).   *(8)*

The Russian Revolution, 1914–33: Seen

The Associated Examining Board Specimen Question Paper 1987

Multiple extract style.   50 marks.   Time allowed: 90 minutes

SECTION A

This section carries 20/100 marks. Study Source Material A and then answer **all** parts of Question 1.

Questions

1

a The author states 9 November (1917); what date would a Russian living at the time give? Why?
(1 mark)

b What viewpoint is associated with the term Cadet (line 25)
(2 marks)

c What can be deduced from the apparent freedom of action of the Cadet newspapers (lines 38–44) concerning the Bolshevik coup?
(3 marks)

d What can be inferred from the author's despatch to the 'Manchester Guardian' (lines 59–71)
(4 marks)

e For what reason can Source A be accepted as reliable?
(4 marks)

f In what ways is Source A helpful in explaining the success of the Bolshevik coup?
(6 marks)

SECTION B

This section carries 30/100 marks. Study Source Materials B1–5 and then answer **all** parts of Question 2.

Questions

2

a Why should Kornilov accuse the Provisional Government of acting with the Germans (Source Material B4, lines 5–6) and Lenin of being a German spy (Source Material B2, lines 4–5)?
(4 marks)

b What is the meaning of the phrase 'a fig-leaf for counter-revolution' (Source Material B2, line 17) as applied to the Soviet?
(5 marks)

c What sources would you need in order to check on the important revelation given in Source B5, lines 9–19?
(3 marks)

d What is the significance of the alleged British aid to Kornilov? (Source Material B1, line 28; and Source Material B2, line 9–11)
(4 marks)

e From the information contained in Sources B and your own knowledge, which of the two secondary sources (B1 or 2) would you regard as the more reliable, and why?
(6 marks)

f Consider the following three interpretations of the Kornilov putsch:

(i) Kornilov acted alone throughout?

(ii) Kornilov and Kerensky acted together against the Soviet and the Bolsheviks, but did not trust each other;

(iii) Kerensky turned to the Soviet and the Bolsheviks because he had failed to control Kornilov in a bid for dictatorship.

Using the evidence presented in Sources B1–5, and your own understanding of the nature of the Kornilov putsch, demonstrate which of the three interpretations is most likely.
(8 marks)

SOURCE MATERIAL A   From M. Philips Price, *Reminiscences of the Russian Revolution*, London, 1921

Study Source Material A and then answer all parts of Question 1.

By November 9th it was clear that power in Petrograd was actually in the hands of the Military Revolutionary Committee, acting in the name of the Second All-Russian Soviet Congress. This all seemed to me at the
5 time very ridiculous, and I wanted to laugh at what had happened in the previous three days. I was still unaccustomed to the atmosphere of Revolution. I tried to imagine a committee of common soldiers and workmen setting themselves up in London and declar-
10 ing that they were the Government, and that no order from Whitehall was to be obeyed unless it was counter-signed by them. I tried to imagine the British Cabinet entering into negotiations with the Committee for the settlement of the dispute, while Buckingham Palace was
15 surrounded by troops and the Sovereign escaped from a side entrance disguised as a washerwoman. And yet something of this sort in Russian surroundings had actually happened. It was almost impossible to realize that the century-old Russian Empire was actually

dissolving before one's eyes with such extraordinary
lack of dignity.

I went down to the Nevskii Prospect on the morning of
the 9th. The middle-class press was being sold in the
streets, as if nothing had happened. Its tone, however,
was muddled. The Cadet *Rech'* appeared too staggered
by the shock to be able to do more than moan about
the fate of Russia. At the Chief Telegraph Office I met a
man who was connected with banking circles. He, too,
was so stunned that he was finding relief by persuading
himself that, although the Bolsheviks had temporarily
succeeded, they could not possibly hold power for
more than a few days. In the Petrograd Telegraph
Agency, however, I found a more confident atmosphere. All the old officials were at work as if nothing had
happened. I was shown telegrams received from what
purported to be soldiers' committees at the front. They
promised every assistance in the task of expelling the
'traitors and usurpers'. Couriers were running backwards
and forwards to the offices of the Cadet newspapers;
leaflets and special anti-Bolshevik bulletins were being
printed and distributed broadcast. It was clear that a
part at least of the bureaucracy, with the intelligentsia
at its head, were already mobilizing against those who
had taken power.

Perhaps, after all, I thought to myself, the whole thing
was a mere adventure. How could committees of
workmen and soldiers, even if they had the passive
consent of the war weary and hungry masses, succeed
against the whole of the technical apparatus of the
bureaucracy and of the agents of foreign finance?

I met an acquaintance who was working with Maxim
Gorky on his newspaper, the *Novaia Zhizn'* 'The
Bolsheviks have made a great mistake in seizing power
by these methods,' he said; 'they cannot possibly hold it
unless the moderate democratic parties come to their
aid.' This view of a Russian progressive intellectual was
very similar to those of outside observers at this time.
'During the weekend,' I wrote in a despatch to the
Manchester Guardian that evening, 'it has been possible
to observe that the right wing of the Bolsheviks are
dissatisfied with the demogogic tactics of Lenin and
Trotsky, who control the new Council of the People's
Commissioners. The only solution giving any hope of
success would be that the moderate peasant parties
should send representatives into the Revolutionary
Government, and thereby exercise a sobering influence.
Within the ranks of the Bolsheviks are differences. The
moderate wing is inclined to the formation of a
Coalition Socialist Ministry. But Lenin and Trotsky
seem intent on turning themselves into cheap editions
of Robespierre.'

SOURCE MATERIAL B

Study Source Materials B1–5 and then answer all parts
of Question 2. All of the Source Material relates to the
Kornilov putsch, August 1917.

SOURCE MATERIAL B1   From M. Liebman, *The
Russian Revolution*, Jonathan Cape, 1970

Many people had the mistaken idea that Kerensky was
defending democracy against reaction. In reality, the
struggle between Kerensky and Kornilov arose not so
much out of political differences as out of political
similarities. While the Right looked upon the Supreme
Commander as a dictator who would save the country
from anarchy Kerensky simply thought that he himself
was the better qualified candidate for that office. His
shift to the Right had been accompanied by the
adoption of an increasingly conservative programme
(discipline, sacrifice, labour) and also by a growing taste
for personal power. ... It is possible that he had all
along intended to turn the Kornilov plot to his own
advantage—in any case he admitted that he had known
of it since the end of the Moscow Conference [15
August]. ... But while Kerensky was more than willing
to make use of Kornilov's services and to include him in
the cabinet, he was not at all disposed to take second
place to him. That was why on August 26, when
Kornilov's true aims could no longer be mistaken, he
ordered him to 'surrender your post'. ... Kornilov was
stunned ... He refused point blank to resign his post,
and in doing so transformed his fight with the Soviet
and the working class into open rebellion against the
Provisional Government. ...

Kornilov, for his part, held yet another trump card: he
enjoyed the confidence of the Allies. Trotsky alleged in
fact, that Britain supplied him with direct aid. ...
Buchanan [British ambassador], in any case, knew all
about the plot but claims that he advised the conspirators to hold back until the Bolsheviks offered them
cause for action.

SOURCE MATERIAL B2   From L. Kochan, *Russia in
Revolution*, Paladin, 1970

Kornilov's rapid rise made him suspect to the Soviet ...
[He] became an early focus for all counter-revolutionary
forces. His programme was simplicity itself. 'The time
has come to hang the German agents and spies, headed
by Lenin' he told his aide-de-camp, 'to disperse the
Soviet of Workers' and Soldiers' Disputes so that it can
never reassemble'. ...

Kornilov's programme attracted some Allied support
and sympathy. In the case of Britain, this extended to

10 finance and the use of a British squadron of armoured
cars . . .

The Kornilov movement, such as it was, ended in a
fiasco, without bloodshed. The very completeness of
this defeat disclosed the basic error in Lenin's analysis
15 of the post-July Soviet. Not only did the Soviet nullify
the idea of a military dictatorship; more important, the
Soviet, supposedly a fig-leaf for counter-revolution,
actually turned itself into a shield against counter-
revolution, even if it also be true that this was only
20 because the latter revealed itself too flagrant and
transparent a guise.

SOURCE MATERIAL B3   Kerensky's telegram to all
the country

I hereby announce:
On August 26 General Kornilov sent . . . a demand for
the surrender by the Provisional Government of all civil
and military power, so that he may form, according to
5 his wishes, a new government to administer the country
. . . [which] was confined subsequently by General
Kornilov in his conversation with me by direct wire . . .

I hereby order:
1. General Kornilov to surrender his post . . .
10 2. The city and uezd of Petrograd to be placed under
martial law . . .

A. F. Kerensky, Minister President, Minister of War and
the Navy, 27 August 1917. As quoted in *Vestnik
Vremennago Pravitelstva*, 29 August 1917

SOURCE MATERIAL B4   Kornilov's response to the
telegram

People of Russia! Our great motherland is dying. The
hour of death is near. Obliged to speak openly, I,
General Kornilov, declare that under the pressure of the
Bolshevik majority in the soviets, the Provisional
5 Government is acting in complete accord with the plans
of the German General Staff, and simultaneously with
the imminent landing of the enemy forces at Riga, it is
destroying the army and is undermining the very
foundations of the country.

General Kornilov, 27 August 1917. As quoted in E. I.
Martynov, *Kornilov*, Leningrad, 1927

SOURCE MATERIAL B5   Memories of U. Kraintsev,
a member in 1917 of the Extraordinary Commission of
Enquiry into the Kornilov putsch

Kornilov catalogued all the measures which the high
command, responsible for waging the war, had proposed to the government in order to rebuild the army
and which that command had adopted itself independ-
5 ently to that end.

Finally, Kornilov came to the most important part, a
part so unexpected that it literally staggered us. He
informed us that in the interests of maintaining order in
the capital he had reached an agreement with Kerensky
10 to move a large military force to Petrograd so that
disturbances, if they occurred, could be suppressed
immediately. It was quite clear from Kornilov's account
that the Soviets (the Soviets of Workers' and Soldiers'
Deputies) were regarded as the main source of the
15 possible disturbances and that by suppression of
disturbances was understood the suppression of none
other than the Soviets and, moreover, that this was so
understood not only in Stavka, but also by Kerensky
himself.

20 To confirm this latter point Kornilov took from a
drawer in his desk a tape with a record of his conversation by direct wire with Kerensky. Unfortunately I
have forgotten when the conversation took place. Each
of us read the tape and, I must confess, we were
25 completely dumbfounded. As the tape revealed, the
main theme of the conversation was the dispatch of the
cavalry force to Petrograd for the purpose which
Kornilov had stated and a purpose which Kerensky's
answers did nothing to contradict . . .

30 There is no proof that Kornilov had a definite plan for
using force not only against the Soviet, but against the
legitimate government as well. . . .

In his letter to this newspaper Kerensky claims that any
idea of a 'pact' is pure invention.

From *Novoye Russkoye Slovo*, New York, 1956

The origins of the Second World War, 1929–39: Seen

University of Cambridge Specimen Paper 1983

Multiple extract style.   25 marks.   Time allowed: 45 minutes

SECTION A

DOCUMENT A   Hitler, *Mein Kampf*, Vol. 2, 1925

The foreign policy of the folkish state must safeguard the existence on this planet of the race embodied in the state, by creating a healthy, viable natural relation between the nation's population and growth on the one
5 hand and the quantity and quality of its soil on the other hand. ... If we speak of soil in Europe today, we can primarily have in mind only Russia and her vassal border states. ... In Russian Bolshevism we must see the attempt undertaken by the Jews in the twentieth
10 century to achieve world domination. ... The fight against Jewish world Bolshevization requires a clear attitude towards Soviet Russia. If today even folkish circles rave about an alliance with Russia, they should just look around them in Germany and see whose
15 support they find in their efforts. Or have folkish men lately begun to view an activity as beneficial to the German people which is recommended and promoted by the international Marxist press? Since when do folkish men fight with armour held out to them by a
20 Jewish squire?

DOCUMENT B   Stalin, Report to the 17th Congress of the Communist Party of the USSR, 26 January 1934

It is not surprising that fascism has now become the most fashionable commodity among war-mongering bourgeois politicians. I am referring not only to fascism in general, but, primarily, to fascism of the German
25 type, which is wrongly called national-socialism – wrongly because the most searching examination will fail to reveal even an atom of socialism in it. ... There have been some changes in the policy of Germany which reflect the growth of revanchist and imperialist
30 sentiments. Some German politicians say that the USSR has now moved to the side of France and Poland; that from an opponent of the Versailles Treaty it has become a supporter of it. That is not true. Our orientation in the past and at the present time is towards the USSR, and
35 towards the USSR alone. ... The point is that Germany's policy has changed. Even before the present German politicians came to power, and particularly after they came to power, a contest began in Germany between two political lines: between the old policy,
40 which was reflected in the treaties between the USSR and Germany, and the 'new' policy of the former German Kaiser, who at one time occupied the Ukraine and marched against Leningrad, after converting the Baltic countries into a base for this march; and this 'new'
45 policy is obviously gaining the upper hand over the old policy.

DOCUMENT C   Molotov–Ribbentrop Agreement, 23 August 1939

The Government of the German Reich and the Government of the Union of Soviet Socialist Republics, directed by the wish to strengthen the cause of peace
50 between Germany and the USSR and proceeding upon the basic provisions of the Treaty of Neutrality concluded between Germany and the USSR in April 1926, have reached the following agreement:

Article 1:
The two contracting parties undertake to refrain from
55 any act of violence, any aggressive action, or any attack against one another, whether individually or jointly with other powers....

Questions

a   Explain the references made in Document A to

  (i) 'the folkish state' (line 1);

  (ii) Russia's 'vassal border states' (lines 7–8);

  (iii) 'Jewish world Bolshevization' (line 11).   *(6)*

b   What light do Documents A and B shed upon the role that ideology played in the attitudes taken by Hitler and Stalin towards international affairs?   *(6)*

c How useful is Stalin's analysis in Document B as an aid to understanding shifts in German policy towards Eastern Europe during the inter-war period? *(6)*

d 'The Molotov–Ribbentrop Pact was the most obvious logical consequence of the Paris Settlement of 1919.' Examine this assertion in the light of these and other documents known to you. *(7)*

The German problem and the peace of Europe: Seen

University of London 1984

Double extract style.   31 marks.   Time allowed: 60 minutes

Study Extracts I and II below and then answer questions **a** to **g** which follow:

EXTRACT I   Four-Power Declaration, July 1957

Twelve years have elapsed since the end of the war in Europe. The hopes of the peoples of the world for the establishment of a basis for a just and lasting peace have nevertheless not been fulfilled. One of the basic
5 reasons for the failure to reach a settlement is the continued division of Germany , which is a grave injustice to the German people and the major source of international tension in Europe.

The governments of France, the United Kingdom and
10 the United States, which share with the Soviet Union responsibility for the reunification of Germany and the conclusion of a peace treaty, and the government of the Federal Republic of Germany , as the only government qualified to speak for the German people as a whole,
15 wish to declare their views on these questions, including the question of European security....

1. ... Justice requires that the German people be allowed to re-establish their national unity on the basis of this fundamental right (to determine their nation's
20 way of life in freedom)....

3. The unnatural division of Germany and of its capital, Berlin, is a continuing source of international tension....

4. Only a freely elected all-German government can undertake on behalf of a reunified Germany obligations
25 which will inspire confidence on the part of other countries....

8. The Western Powers have never required as a condition of German reunification that a reunified Germany should join the North Atlantic Treaty
30 Organisation. It will be for the people of ... Germany themselves to determine ... whether they wish to share in the benefits and obligations of the treaty....

11. The reunification of Germany accompanied by the conclusion of European security arrangements would
35 facilitate the achievement of a comprehensive disarmament agreement.

EXTRACT II   President Kennedy, July 1961

Our presence in West Berlin, and our access thereto, cannot be ended by any act of the Soviet government. The NATO shield was long ago extended to cover
40 West Berlin. ... For West Berlin, lying exposed 110 miles inside East Germany, surrounded by Soviet troops and close to Soviet supply lines, has many roles. It is more than a showcase of liberty, a symbol, an island of freedom in a Communist sea. It is even more than a link
45 with the free world, a beacon of hope behind the Iron Curtain, an escape hatch for refugees.

West Berlin is all of that. But above all it has now become, as never before, the great testing place of Western courage and will , a focal point where our
50 solemn commitments, stretching back over the years since 1945, and Soviet ambitions now meet in basic confrontation....

We cannot and will not permit the Communists to drive us out of Berlin, either gradually or by force.

Questions (Maximum marks)

a (i) Explain *each* of the terms, 'Iron Curtain' (lines 46) and 'NATO shield' (line 39)

(ii) What name is commonly used for 'the Federal Republic of Germany' (line 13), and who was its Chancellor at the time of both of these Extracts? *(4)*

b Explain how the four powers named in lines 9–10 had come to 'share' 'responsibility for' Germany, and how 'our presence in West Berlin' (line 37) had first come about. *(4)*

c 'Escape hatch for refugees' (line 46): how was this hatch closed within months of the address by Kennedy which is quoted in Extract II? *(2)*

d Explain on what earlier occasion West Berlin had proved a 'great testing place of Western courage and will' (lines 48–49), and how the West had then demonstrated it would not be driven 'out of Berlin' (line 54). *(3)*

e How had the 'division of Germany' come to be 'continued' (line 6) by the time of the Declaration quoted in Extract I, and how far should the blame for this division be attributed to 'Soviet ambitions' (line 51)? *(6)*

f What evidence of Western propaganda related to the Cold War would a sympathiser with the Soviet Union be likely to find in each of these Extracts? *(5)*

g Assess what progress had been made by 1975 towards 'the reunification of Germany', 'European security arrangements' and 'disarmament agreement' (lines 33–36) *(7)*